Emotional Intelligence *for* Emerging Leaders *and* Entrepreneurs

- Illustrating the Fortune Giants

Emotional Intelligence *for* Emerging Leaders *and* Entrepreneurs

- Illustrating the Fortune Giants

SEHBA HUSAIN

PARTRIDGE

A Penguin Random House Company

To order additional copies of this book, contact
Partridge India
000 800 10062 62
orders.india@partridgepublishing.com

www.partridgepublishing.com/india

Contents

Dedicated to

My father Mr. A. Shakoor Khan and my children Fatima and Yousuf, who are great emotional strength to me!

Foreword

I have seen number of entrepreneurs struggling hard to achieve their business goals especially those who have small, medium or newly started business enterprises. Their major area of concern remains how to sell their products successfully to the consumers and increase the volume of sales to earn required profits. Also, they face number of issues pertaining to productivity, performance and behavior of their employees. Moreover, they have to often face financial crunch due to non availability of investors or their disengagement with the business. Serious issues are sometimes raised by government authorities, non government organizations to favor communities and society. Third parties like suppliers and distributors also seem to lose the sync with the business now and then. After having close assessment of these challenges, I discovered one single reason behind all such sort of business problems. It is Lack of use of Emotional Intelligence (EI) in making business decisions.

Purpose of this book is to provide help to new and emerging leaders and entrepreneurs enabling them to achieve their bottomline in most efficient manner. Various integrated models and frameworks have been developed with the motive to:

> ➤ Make leaders and entrepreneurs understand the meaning of EI and its value to manage people associated with their business;

> ➤ Empower them with the tools to implement EI based strategies which help them manage marketing, increase sales, manage employee's productivity, performance and behavior and ensure high level stakeholders engagement for business success.

To provide appropriate benchmark, five corporations that are listed in Fortune 500 list of global companies have been taken as instance of some of the most emotional intelligent corporations. Information of these corporations has been drawn from different online sources like their annual reports, sustainability reports, websites, blogs, news etc. This information has been used under the provision of 'fair use' of intellectual property rights framework developed by WIPO (World Intellectual Property Organization). These corporations have been selected as great instance of 'Emotional Intelligent Companies' who have made it to great global success by implementing EI based strategies to manage all their direct and indirect stakeholders. I hope this book will serve its purpose to its fullest by facilitating leaders to master the art of using EI to achieve most sustainable business growth.

I am thankful to Mr. Allan Gatenby, leadership and career management expert for support he provided throughout this project. His vision of leadership is unique and his expertise is second to none when it comes to deliver coaching and mentoring support in various areas of leadership, change management, individual and organizational effectiveness. I am also grateful to Dr. Michael Petty, strategic business foresight and leadership expert who helped me to extend my knowledge by sharing his outstanding perspectives on business models and relevance of EI for the same. He helped me immensely on my trip to the USA that empowered me further to develop the cross cultural insights in EI.

Inspiration for this work I received from the work of Daniel Goleman which influenced me to probe more into the fundamental and specific concepts of EI. In July 2013, I undertook the online course 'Inspiring Leadership through Emotional Intelligence' by Richard E. Boyatzis, another pioneer in the field of Emotional Intelligence. His course enabled me to develop outstanding acumen in resonant leadership and coaching with compassion. In March 2014, I got the opportunity to take 'MSCEIT Certification' through 'MSCEIT Certification and EI Skill Building Workshop' conducted by David Caruso. He inspired me to the great extent by his knowledge and expertise in the area of EI and its application in various contexts. He is the one who demonstrates great EI skills through his behavior along with having deep and most useful knowledge of this intelligence. I express my gratitude to all these experts and pioneers in EI and leadership for exerting great influence and inspiring me to complete this work with better developed perspectives and insights. Finally and most importantly I am thankful to almighty and then my family for being highly supportive to me and being my strength to do and achieve whatever I want in my life.

An Overview

With changes happening almost every next moment with economic and social systems across the nations, emotional intelligence (EI) is gaining more importance and becoming a significant area of study for researchers and scholars worldwide. Concept of EI is directly associated with the field of psychology and has influence over number of spheres wherever 'human' factor is involved. When we talk about business and its management, human factor is a must to be considered at priority as business is all about people. It is of the people, for the people and by the people.

Emotional intelligence deals with understanding, interpreting and then managing the emotions of self and others. Study of EI is not centuries old. This concept was first quoted in the work of Wayne Payne (1985) in his doctorate dissertation. Then in 1990, two psychologists Peter Salovey and John Mayer published a revolutionary research article titled 'Emotional Intelligence' which had paved the way for scholars, researchers and writers in the related areas of EI. Daniel Goleman has pioneered the area of emotional intelligence by his researches and writings on EI. He did not only give concrete views on significance of EI in the areas of leadership and performance effectiveness but also has suggested strong models applicable to productivity improvements.

Earlier, intellectual capacity of a person was measured in terms of effectiveness of his Intelligence Quotient (IQ). More logical skills you have more you would be perceived as intelligent and competent. Scholars in the area of psychology have proved that IQ is not only criteria for effective performance but other types of intelligences also play important role in how you perform and excel area you are associated with. As discussed by Howard Gardener[1] there are nine kinds of intelligences associated with a human personality. These are:

1. Naturalist Intelligence ("Nature Smart")
2. Musical Intelligence ("Musical Smart")
3. Logical-Mathematical Intelligence ("Number/Reasoning Smart")
4. Existence Intelligence
5. Bodily-Kinesthetic Intelligence ("Body Smart")
6. Linguistic Intelligence ("Word Smart")
7. Spatial Intelligence ("Picture Smart")
8. Intra-personal Intelligence ("Self Smart")
9. Interpersonal Intelligence ("People Smart")

Last two types of intelligences can best define 'emotional intelligence' of a person. Intra personal intelligence refers to the understanding the 'self'. The extent to which you can understand your own purpose, characteristics, priorities, likes and dislikes, motives, ambitions, strengths, limitations and weaknesses and finally the approach to manage your 'self'. This ability to understand and manage your 'self' constitutes your intra personal intelligence. On the other hand, interpersonal intelligence constitutes person's intelligence to understand process and regulate emotions of people he is dealing with. Fundamentally, interpersonal intelligence help person to understand other's personality, likes and dislikes, motives and approaches to manage other's behaviour in different situations.

Where emotional intelligence refers to person's intelligence to understand, interpret and regulate emotions of self and others, emotional quotient (EQ) is the term associated with measurement of emotional intelligence and is the main EI measurement unit. As a matter of fact, emotional quotient is a term that determines person's level of EI which is often represented as the score in a standardized EI test. Number of EI tests are developed to measure person's EQ by testing his response under various situations. Some of the popular tests that measure person's emotional intelligence are:

• Mayer-Salovey-Caruso Emotional Intelligence Test (MSCEIT);
• Yale's Emotional Intelligence Test;
• Emotional and Social Competency Inventory (ESCI)

Scientific View of Emotional Intelligence

Simply saying, an emotion can be considered as the driving force of all behavior including motivation in its positive and negative terms. It is a subjective and a conscious experience that can be characterized by psychophysiological expressions, mental states and biological (bodily) reactions.[2] All our sense organs eyes, nose, skin, tongue and ears receive the sensory inputs which then are transferred to the significant parts of brain where these inputs are processed and convert into particular emotions. In complex vertebrates including humans, emotional reactions are processed in amygdala. The almond shaped structures located in temporal lobes of human brain, amygdalae are responsible for persons social and emotional functioning in brain.

During a specific emotional episode, a person passes sequence of events. According to Scherer following components coordinate together to create an emotional experience for an organism:[3]

- Cognitive appraisal: provides an evaluation of events and objects
- Bodily symptoms: the physiological component of emotional experience
- Action tendencies: a motivational component for the preparation and direction of motor responses.
- Expression: facial and vocal expression almost always accompanies an emotional state to communicate reaction and intention of actions

- Feelings: the subjective experience of emotional state once it has occurred

Emotions can be categorized as positive and negative emotions. Positive emotions like affection, love, joy, happiness, confidence, satisfaction, gratitude etc. make person feel good moods and have positive experiences. On the contrary negative emotions like anger, annoyance, disgust, frustration, grief, anxiety, hatred, sorrow, worry etc. make person feel sad and experience bad moods.

Though considered as mental states, emotions are directly linked to the physiological health and responses too. When positive emotions are felt by a human being, he tends to think more rationally and logically. He acts in more thoughtful manner which makes his behavior more socially acceptable and productive. On the other hand, when negative emotions are felt by an individual, his body starts secreting different hormones which shut down his cognitive and rational thinking abilities. He then starts behaving the ways that sometimes even decline his social acceptance. This is the reason why it is considered that emotions are responsible for human's behavior and performance in all his personal and professional life settings.

Emotional intelligence in human beings helps them to manage behavior by regulating various positive and negative emotions. Even when come across most negative emotions, an emotional intelligent person tries to counter the negative effects of situation by understanding the consequences of his positive or negative response to stimuli. It is therefore emotional intelligence that drives a person's behavior and has direct significance on success he achieves in different spheres of his life.

Behavioral View of Emotional Intelligence

Though captured attention few decades back, concept of emotional intelligence is not an absolutely new area of study. Emotional intelligence has been an important and basic type of intellectual ability possessed by human beings since they came into existence and developed more as they started getting civilized. Ages back too people used to live in pairs and groups in order to fulfill their sexual and social needs. While interacting with each other they developed senses of liking, loving and caring for each other.

Theories of evolution and learning say that it is human's tendency that he learns from his experiences and improves the ways he responds to different stimuli in different situations. There is still great debate on question whether emotional intelligence could be learnt or not? This is true that most of the fundamental intelligences are gifted to human beings by nature but person also takes birth with the great quality of 'learning with experiences' and hence both nature and nurture components have great influence over emotional intelligence of a person.

As discussed before, emotional intelligence consists of person's interpersonal and intrapersonal abilities to regulate emotions to manage desired behavior. If it is not the case of neutral behavior which is characterized by neither showing positive nor negative response, a person is likely to show either the positive or the negative behavior to a particular stimuli (situation).

Behavior is not only the outcome of emotions person feels at a specific situation but it is also the result of concept he develops of that situation. Such concept, positive and negative is developed by him on the basis of his experiences, perceptions, background and his individual personality. Even when coming across the most positive situation some people end up behaving most negative way due to their self concept that determines their behavior in different situations. Let us take the example of general interaction of two people in negotiation and see in the following table how this concept works:

Table 1

	Positive Behavior (Outcome of Positive Concept Development)	**Negative Behavior (Outcome of Negative Concept Development)**
Feelings Depicted	Satisfaction, happiness, contentment, agreement etc.	Dissatisfaction, sadness, discontentment, disagreement etc.
Communication	Favorable – depicted in positive speech, body language and facial expressions	Not Favorable – depicted in negative speech, body language and facial expressions
Approach	Constructive – Tries to create win-win situation	Destructive – Tries to create win-lose situation
Outcome	Interaction usually successful in achieving desired goals of both the parties	Interaction usually fails in achieving desired goals of both the parties

Other than the self concept, motives also play significant role in shaping the human behavior. Motive can be considered as the reward person expects from a specific interaction, situation, object or an action. In social settings, whenever people interact with each other they interact with certain motive and then shape behavior following a structured process. Interaction could be preplanned intentional attempt or it can be an unplanned, unintentional event. In both the situations person shapes his behavior keeping his motives in view and follows a structured process with following five stages:

1. Encountering (person or situation)
2. Understanding motives (self and others)
3. Developing Concepts (positive vs. negative)
4. Regulating Emotions (in accordance with self motives)
5. Shaping the Behavior (positive or negative)

When person comes across or encounters the other person, he gives a thought to whether motives of that person are aligned and synced to his own motives or not. If he finds motives of encountering party benefiting him achieve his own motives he regulates his emotions to shape positive behavior characterized by a healthy conversation, positive gestures and body language, content facial expressions, sharing of thoughts and productive approach resulting the desired behavior outcome.

Contrary to this, if person finds encountering party's motives not aligned to his own motives, not beneficial for him, or may cause harm to him, he develops negative concepts, regulates his emotions to shape his behavior the negative way characterized by ignorance, disagreement, and other undesirable behaviors.

Motives are drivers of human behavior. As discussed above human behavior depends highly upon motives person has in his mind. In his daily course of life person goes through two types of interactions – formal interactions and informal interactions. Formal interactions are related to one's profession life whereas informal interactions are related to his personal life. We know that being professional whenever people interact they interact with motives but in fact, in personal life too whenever people interact they interact with motives. These personal motives could aim at attaining personal satisfaction from relationships like from spouse, friends and even our community. We try to fulfill our mental and physical desires from our near and dear ones and these desires are our motives. Human behavior fundamentally depends upon the intensity and valence of these motives. If motive is something that affects our life to great extent, we will focus to attain that motive by shaping our behavior more positively and mindfully. On the other hand if motive does not contribute to anything great in your life, you will not give much emphasis to keep your behavior exactly positive and will behave as situation demands.

New sales executive George, in his first month of job has been given a target to sell at least 5000 units of particular product. He is in his probation period and his performance for this month will decide his further existence in the job. To sell 5000 units of a product the executive has to meet 5000 people in a month i.e. around 227 people per day (if he works 22 days a month). In order to reach to his target he needs to meet people in the market, offer the product by communicating with clients specifying all features of the product and finally make successful sale. In all the interactions and meetings every day, he has to manage his behavior with lot of patience, tolerance and positive expressions because intensity of his motive *'I want to save my job'* is quite high. Last day of the month he is left with 10 more sales to accomplish his target and it was already 8'O clock in the evening, people were not responding well in the market as this is the time of market to close down. He is frustrated, tensed when a woman comes to him asking series of the questions about the product.

To each question of hers he is responding positively with polite answers and good expressions. Finally she did not buy product and left. Sooner, another salesman comes to George, offering him shaving cream hamper at lowest cost. As soon as that salesman tried to take offer further, George shouted badly on him and vents all his anger refusing his offer before its completion. Why George despite of being frustrated, tired and worried behaves positively to a woman asking unnecessary questions? And why he got annoyed with the salesman who is simply offering him a good product? Answer lies in 'motives'. End of the day George had still to make 10 sales to save his job and lady who came to him though asked many unnecessary questions was giving George the ray of hope that he will successfully sell his products to her. His motive drives him to shape his behavior in positive way whereas in case of that salesman George was not at all interested in buying that shaving cream hamper, valence of motive in salesman case was absolutely low and hence he exhibited his worst behavior to that salesman which was outburst of his accumulated frustration.

Emotionally intelligent people understand their motives well and shape their behavior in most appropriate ways. But managing your own behavior is not sufficient. You must know how to manage other's behavior. Though it is not that easy task, you can do it by winning their positive consideration through strong influence of your personality. Now question arises what do I mean by influencing or good personality? What are the criteria? As a matter of fact personality having good weight attracts people. Yes, there is the weightage of personality that attracts people. We respect people usually because we like them for some of the important features or traits of their personality. These features could also be considered as components of personality. A human being contains certain physical and psychological traits that combinedly create a 'personality'. Physical traits of such type include person's physical appearance, beauty, height, weight, complexion, physique and overall looks which leave great influence on human's mind. Further non physical components of personality include person's social status, qualification, designation, financial status, relationships and his ability to influence others i.e. his personal behavior and attitude, his emotional intelligence. EI is considered to be one of the important personality traits that influence human behavior.

An emotional intelligent person manages his and others behavior to get his tasks done and achieve his goals in most efficient way. It is evident from the history that leaders with outstanding personality have proven to be the most effective ones when it comes to influencing the masses. In the next section we will see how leaders with great emotional intelligence ruled the people around the world through the ages.

Great Leaders and EI

Prophet Mohammad

Prophet Mohammad was born in Arabia in the year 570 C.E. He took birth though in a very well reputed clan of Arabia 'Quraish' he was the orphan since his birth and had lost his mother at the age of six. He was illiterate and worked as a shepherd in his initial years. He started his mission of preaching and spreading Islam at the age of 40. He died at the age of 63 and during this short period of 23 years he transformed entire Arabian society and influenced uncountable people around the world. Today Islam is considered to be the second most practicing religion of the world just due to teachings and influence of Prophet Mohammad's personality.

Before Mohammad, Arabs were considered to be most barbaric, adamant, aggressive, and violent people. Practices of paganism and idolatry were common in Arabia. Tribal quarrels, drunkenness, women abuse, lawlessness and debauchery were plaguing Arabian society. With his emotional intelligence, worthy advices and strong communication skills Mohammad disciplined Arabs and brought miraculous change to entire society.

Some of the personality traits of Prophet Mohammad prove him to have high levels of emotional intelligence and they are:

He used to observe people's pattern of behavior before taking decisions. He always talked about goodness, charity, justice, peace, discipline, forgiveness and mercy, everything in favor of mankind that helped him to create a highly appreciable personality when people were suffering disorders of unsystematic ways of living.

He had amazing capability to communicate. He was very eloquent and spoke whenever really required. His speech was understandable, comprehensible and very well structured. His tone was sweetest and most favorable and he never used evil words against anyone. By way of Quran he taught people about the reality and existence of '*ALLAH*' the Almighty in Islam. He knew very well the worsening social scenario that time and knew what people want there in Arabia, he knew what strategies will work there and how to make people ready to follow his path. He first understood and defined his own goals, his motive that was transformation of Arab society. Based on the motives of people then he shaped his strategy to take Arabs in unity. That time common motive of most of the Arabs was 'peace' because of prevalence of quarrels and lawlessness amongst various tribes.

Prophet Mohammad devised the strategy as per which he made first, a team of a few people who first accepted him as a prophet of Allah. With that team then he started spreading the message of Allah about 'values of life'. He used to invite people, would personally meet them and tell the importance of Islam and its teachings. As discussed earlier he had a charismatic personality with very soft tone of speech due to which people used to get highly attracted to him and would accepted whatever he suggest.

Great Scholar George Bernard Shaw told about Prophet Mohammad ...

"I believe that if a man like him were to assume the dictatorship of the modern world he would succeed in solving its problems in a way that would bring it the much needed peace and happiness: I have prophesied about the faith of Muhammad that it would be acceptable to the Europe of tomorrow as it is beginning to be acceptable to the Europe of today."[4]

Bernard Shaw appreciated Prophet Mohammad for his legitimate leadership. He even thought that with Mohammad's approaches problems of modern European society could be solved in easiest way.

Prof. K.S Ramakrishna Rao considered Prophet Mohammad, "Perfect Model for Human Life" in his book 'Muhammad, the Prophet of Islam' he said –

"The personality of Muhammad, it is most difficult to get into the whole truth of it. Only a glimpse of it I can catch. What a dramatic succession of picturesque scenes! There is Muhammad, the Prophet. There is Muhammad, the Warrior; Muhammad, the Businessman; Muhammad, the Statesman; Muhammad, the Orator; Muhammad, the Reformer; Muhammad, the Refuge of Orphans; Muhammad, the Protector of Slaves; Muhammad, the Emancipator of Women; Muhammad, the Judge; Muhammad, the Saint. All in all these magnificent roles, in all these departments of human activities, he is alike a hero."[5]

Mahatma Gandhi viewed character of Muhammad as (Said in Young India):

"I wanted to know the best of one who holds today's undisputed sway over the hearts of millions of mankind....I became more than convinced that it was not the sword that won a place for Islam in those days in the scheme of life. It was the rigid simplicity, the utter self-effacement of the Prophet, the scrupulous regard for his pledges, his intense devotion to this friends and followers, his intrepidity, his fearlessness, his absolute trust in God and in his own mission.

These and not the sword carried everything before them and surmounted every obstacle. When I closed the 2nd volume (of the Prophet's biography), I was sorry there was not more for me to read of the great life."[6]

It is clear from great Gandhi's sayings that Mohammad did not use sword to win the battle of wisdom but he used his intellect, his emotional intelligence in form of non violence, love, peace, communication and brotherhood. Mohammad was a man of high emotional intelligence that helped him to understand motives of self and society and manage the behavior of people not only of Arab peninsula but millions of people across the world.

Mahatma Gandhi (Mohan Das Karamchand Gandhi) himself was an extraordinary influencing leader. He fought for independence against 200 years of British rule in India and succeeded with his powerful strategy of non violence and non cooperation. He was a great visionary, knew what his people want and what is the intensity of that need, that motive. 'Freedom' was something every Indian of that time strongly desired. Regardless of religion, caste and class, people came together under leadership of Mahatma Gandhi, fought and won independence in the year 1947. Before Mahatma Gandhi, number of leaders came with their views, approaches and initiatives but no one could, at a time influence such a huge mass which would work for single goal with one approach of non cooperation and non violence. India since inception is a land of great diversity. People from different regions, religions, colors and castes live just as - Indians. But that time each community had its own fundamental principles and approaches to fight for freedom. People from some specific communities were more inclined toward leaders who originated from their own communities and regions. For example the Mahars (untouchables) would respect and follow Dr. Bhimrao Ambedkar, who stood against discrimination for untouchables.

Similarly Muslims respected Muslim league leaders like Mohammad Ali Jinnah and Dr. Mohammad Iqbal and people from Tamil Nadu used to follow C.R. Periyyar who was inclined towards Tamili fundamentals. Bengalis were influenced by the thoughts of Subhash Chandra Bose whereas Maharashtrians adored Vinayek Savarkar. Mahatma Gandhi on the other hand has been considered as the most influential leader of that time as Indians from almost all regions, religions, communities, castes and all classes got influenced from his ideologies of freedom. Why his ideology was accepted and appreciated by these many people from different communities and regions? He developed his ideologies with great emotional intelligence. He did not ask people to sacrifice their lives and fight with violence in battlefield. He knew human emotions, and hence the value of human life, human well being, and human relations due to which he came up with policy of just not to cooperate with British Government in any manner, any dealings. He used strong tool of non violence which was considerable and possible to adopt by society at large.

Mahatma Gandhi presented his motive to public in most intelligent way. Well researched, structured, developed, very well communicated and evaluated for its consequences. As we are emphasizing continuously on the fact that success of leadership is determined by strength of motives and ability to communicate motives and managing self and others' behavior, Mahatma Gandhi could be perceived as one of the best instances of such leaders who won the battle with all these strong tools.

Gandhi's policy of non violence proved that strong that it influenced number of great leaders to work upon his footsteps. In 1959 great Martin Luther King Junior visited India. He was highly inspired by Gandhi's non violence approach and based his movement of civil rights on the same fundamentals of struggle for freedom without use of violence in America.

Born on January 15, 1929 in Atlanta, Georgia, Martin Luther King still is considered as one of world's greatest leaders. He had high capability to understand and work according to the emotional requirements of people. He played pivotal role in ending racial discrimination and legal segregation of Africans in America. Among several other honors he received Nobel Peace Prize in 1964 for his commendable approach toward equality amongst people of all colors and races.

Martin Luther King Jr. ruled hearts of millions of people by communicating his strong message of equality and peace in the most efficient way. That time in America there was a strong discrimination amongst Americans and African American people. Negros had to face great disappointment and humiliation due to segregation policies of the states which prohibited Negros to express political views, attend schools where white students would study, meeting white people and even to vote. Their situation was extremely bad as most of them were living their lives with curse of poverty, slavery and discrimination. Martin Luther King who himself studied in segregated school, wanted to cure the problem from the root.

Highly inspired from Indian revolution for freedom ignited by Mohandas Karamchand Gandhi, King decided to pave path with same strong approach of curing problem with emotions management. He appealed Negros to come together for their rights, to raise their voices, to fight for freedom. Finally, Civil Rights Act of 1964 and the Voting Rights Act of 1965 passed by Government to protect rights of African-American people in America. King used great emotional intelligence tools of understanding problem, managing own and others motives, communicating the solutions and getting them administered right time right way. His great power to communicate reflects in his popular speech 'I have a dream' which he delivered to address people emphasizing 'America free of discrimination', Negros happy and equal as other races of America. Speech influenced great number of people around the world and resulted revolution across the nations for African race's peace and equality.

Apart from leaders who established instances in spreading religion, fights against slavery and injustice and for independence and equality let us now talk about leaders who left seismic impact of their emotional intelligence in the world of business and trade. In this context we have almost thousands of leaders to talk about. Almost all successful business leaders are driven by high levels of emotional intelligence which helps them to manage their most important factor of business – Manpower.

"If there is any one secret of success, it lies in the ability to get the other person's point of view and see things from that person's angle as well as from your own."[7]

- Henry Ford
Founder Ford Motors

With his great vision Henry Ford propelled his business to highest levels of success. He came up with a revolutionary concept of assembly line production, and managed change in the most efficient way. As a matter of fact every success is an outcome of some sort of revolution. May it be on personal level, societal level, organizational level or national level, change can never be managed without harnessing revolution amongst people in concerned community of people. Henry Ford was a great visionary with capability to manage people's emotions. With his perfect communication skills he accelerated the idea of introduction of change in production process. He brought revolution of new production process – Assembly line in his automobile plant which gave his business new heights of eternal success. Today that process has become the fundamental technique of production in various types of industries.

> *Success needs change, change needs revolution, and revolution needs people – driven by high EMOTIONAL INTELLIGENCE*

Not only Ford, but number of leaders has proven how emotional intelligence can be used as powerful tool of competitive advantage. Using emotional intelligence as a tool for business success doesn't only focus on taking care of feelings of employees but it emphasizes on concern for emotions of all stakeholders which finally consist of human element. Tata group in India corroborate welfare of people irrespective of their stake in Tata's business. This group of companies is known for its initiatives in area of public welfare and upliftment of weaker sections of society. The 'people concerned' image of Tata has helped the group to sustain a super positive image over long period of time.

Maruti, one of the most successful automobile giant in India, is known for its strong customer satisfaction strategies. Maruti's strategies focus on almost every aspect that can result in high level of customer loyalty. Company manufactures different cars for people belong to various income levels, individual preferences, age groups etc. what is more important for them is – to what extent customer is delighted using Maruti product i.e The Car.

Sam Walton, founder of Walmart chain of stores would also be one of the best examples to discuss in this context.

"The secret of successful retailing is to give your customers what they want. And really, if you think about it from your point of view as a customer, you want everything: a wide assortment of good-quality merchandise; the lowest possible prices; guaranteed satisfaction with what you buy; friendly, knowledgeable service; convenient hours; free parking; a pleasant shopping experience."[8]

- Sam Walton
Founder Walmart

Walmart is considered to be one of the most successful companies of all times and has declared world's number one global company in 2011. Company has ranked number one on the FORTUNE 500 list for four years in a row. Its success is totally based upon satisfaction stores provide to their customers. Company's three basic values consist of respect for the individual, service to customers and strive for excellence, all focused upon the 'customer'. Company devises all possible strategies that can give customers great shopping experience and value for their money. Sam Walton believed that because people work hard for every dollar, they deserve the lowest price Walmart can offer every time customer makes purchase. His service philosophies confirmed long run profits with high customer loyalty for Walmart stores. He understood that people want highest satisfaction from money they spend on their purchases.

Walton decided to cater to needs of customers belong to all income levels by offering products branded, unbranded, expensive, cheaper, discounted and even if customer doesn't like product he can return product back or can exchange it. Company's approach toward customers value ensures its international success which also proves corporate strategies highly emotion focused.

It is very much appropriate to say that strategies focused on the 'emotion' element of human stakeholders of business ensure long term success of the business. It is finally emotions of human beings that make them loyal toward specific business entity. Be it employees, customers, shareholders or society at large, every section needs to have their expectations fulfilled by business they are relying upon. Satisfaction of expectations positively motivates emotions of person to stay loyal for that business and brand.

Emotional Intelligence in Business

Emotional Intelligence as explained earlier constitutes a person's intrapersonal and interpersonal intelligence. In context of business hence emotional intelligence of a business concern can be divided as:

Intrapersonal Business intelligence: Intrapersonal business intelligence is the acumen of entrepreneurs to have complete knowledge of their business - their own capabilities, resources, vision, mission, values, goals & objectives, strengths, weaknesses, opportunities, threats and also other environment factors that may influence their business functioning.

Interpersonal Business Intelligence: This intelligence on the other hand deals with business's relationship with all its direct and indirect stakeholders. Be it entrepreneurs or promoters, employees, customers, suppliers, distributors, investors or even society at large, business needs to focus on having good understanding of what these stakeholders expect from the business and what will result in managing good relationship with them to ensure sustainable business success.

Businesses functioning with good emotional intelligence of decision makers (interpersonal and intrapersonal) know what they stand for, where they stand, how and why they stand, when (the time) they stand in the marketplace and what their stakeholders want from them. Corporations hence right from setting their vision, mission, goal and objectives stay focused on how they will be able to offer maximum emotional value to its stakeholders and to themselves too.

Emotional value can be defined as the ability of particular material or non material object, situation or event to generate positive emotions to be felt by a human being. For example: Material object like a car, a laptop or non material objects like a piece of music, a composition, a song, a poem that makes you feel happy and satisfied have got positive and higher emotional value. Opposite to this if you buy a watch that after buying you find does not worth what you spend on that have negative emotional value. In logical terms it would be appropriate to say that emotional value is the value of your satisfaction of emotions over your value of expenditure. Expenditure may be in terms of money, time or even effort.

So it can be expressed as:

Emotional Value = Value of Satisfied Emotions/Value of Expenditure

Hence, if value of satisfied emotions is more than the expenditure the emotional value would be positive and opposite to this, when value of satisfied emotions is less than the expenditure, emotional value would be negative.

We can better understand the crux of emotional value with the help of 'Emotional Value Continuum and FEN Model' which integrates 'Feelings', 'Emotions' and 'Needs' of a person together to know how emotional value is generated by intricacy of these three elements. In the model 'F' stands for feelings, 'E' stands for emotions and 'N' stands for needs. It is assumed that emotional value of something may it be a material or non material object, situation or event is generated, grown, or reduced due to the relevance of needs, feelings felt and emotions experienced while coming across the situation, event or object.

The model is developed on the foundation principles of Maslow's hierarchy of needs. In the model, the pyramid is composed of three levels. The bottom level shows that person experiences 'good' feelings and 'satisfaction' as emotion when his 'basic needs' get fulfilled. Second level enunciates the 'comfort needs' (needs), 'satisfaction and happiness' (emotions) and better (feelings) which demonstrates that when person's comfort needs get fulfilled he feels better and along with satisfaction he also experience the sense of happiness. Finally at top section of pyramid there are 'luxury and self actualization needs' (needs), 'satisfaction, happiness and pride' (emotions) and best (feelings). This stage reveals that when person's luxury and self actualization needs get fulfilled he feels the best and experience emotions that are satisfaction, happiness and pride. Following table helps understand the assumption in a right manner.

Table 2

Levels (from Bottom)	Example (Situation)	Needs Fulfilled	Feelings Felt	Emotions Experienced
I	A beggar gets loaf of bread and he eats that.	Basic	Good	Satisfaction
II	Student got bike to commute to his school.	Comfort	Better	Satisfaction and happiness
III	Wife received a diamond ring from husband as wedding anniversary gift.	Luxury and Self Actualization	Best	Satisfaction, Happiness and Pride

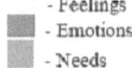 - Feelings
- Emotions
- Needs

EV = Emotional Value

Figure 1 Emotional Value Continuum and FEN Model

Emotional value is assumed to be increasing from neutral to good to better to best and decreasing from neutral to bad to worse to worst. So for example if one person having limited money is hungry, he feels good when he finds a street vendor selling burgers affordable to him. But if he also is offered by vendor, a complimentary coke then it makes him feel better and finally when he gets offered a table to have his meal in an air conditioned room by the side of street, he feels the best and this is how his emotional value for meal keeps on increasing from neutral to best. Underlying assumption here is advanced the level of needs fulfilled, more positive emotions are felt by human being. This is the reason why business entities providing goods and services of basic needs, try to be able to satisfy even higher order needs of their consumers.

In context of business, emotional value continuum and FEN model can be associated with building brand image. Nowadays it is not surprising to see daily needs or basic needs products being sold in better, comfortable packaging, carry differentiated unique features and hold a good brand name. Bisleri, the bottled water owned by Parle Bisleri pvt. Ltd is a good example of how corporations achieve success focusing onto increasing emotional value of the product. Water - product that fulfills basic need is packed in attractive bottles, added minerals, also holds a good brand name provides customers with great emotional contentment. With its huge distribution, water is comfortably available almost everywhere and its unique contents, added minerals and reputed brand name make person feel proud to be the consumer of that product.

In markets there are innumerable products available that focus on fulfilling consumers basic, comfort, luxury and self actualization needs. It is however different from consumer to consumer that what products are appropriate to fulfill his different set of needs. For example, Samsung galaxy tablet for a rich adolescent is a product that satisfies his comfort need but for adolescent who belong to a poor family this would be a product that fulfils his luxury needs as he belongs to a different segment of society. Companies as a matter of fact do proper market analysis before implementing any product idea to action. Market analysis helps corporations to study market well and make segmentation on various parameters. Social class element is always taken into consideration while segmenting the market whereby it is decided that what social class (top, middle or lower) is appropriate to target. After deciding upon the segment companies make efforts to produce and offer goods that generate great emotional value and satisfy almost all levels of needs of consumers they target at specific period of time.

It is therefore mandatory for organizations nowadays to keep focused on emotional value of their offering right from the stage of setting their vision, mission, values, goals and objectives. Companies cannot survive nowadays without applying emotional intelligence in business decisions as it has become an imperative for them to follow EI principles that help them achieve long term sustainable growth.

Since emotional intelligence can be learned and developed it can and should be managed in a way that it will be able to contribute great to the business success. Businesses can plan to be emotional intelligent, they can organize, direct, and control to have various levels of this intelligence. Managing EI is mandatory for business success and in the following sections various approaches and concepts that integrate business success with EI, are discussed in more detailed manner.

Stakeholder Approach to Manage EI for Business Success

The Stakeholder Approach to manage emotional intelligence for business is a twofold doctrine. It is about first, business's intellect and ability to understand and develop knowledge of the significance, depth and requirements of its own vision, mission, goals and objectives. Second, use that knowledge to devise strategies based upon EI principles for maximum stakeholders' support. May it be the key stakeholders like entrepreneurs (including promoters, board of directors, business owners and founders), employees, customers, investors and shareholders or the indirect stakeholders like societies and environment, business needs proper underpinning by all these parties to function together toward achieving business goals in highly dynamic business environment. Hence, the stakeholders approach enunciates business' strategies and initiatives that help it to attract the emotions of its stakeholders to ensure their absolute and maximum support to business. It includes all initiatives businesses use to captivate positive attention of employees, investors, consumers, governments and even societies to accomplish business goals and objectives.

Business is a complex system, outcome of stakes and efforts of number of parties having vested interests in that business. These stakeholders' support actually determines how efficiently business operates, implements strategies, earns profits, sustains growth and development and further expands.

Entrepreneurs, investors, employees, consumers, communities and society are important stakeholders of business comprising of 'human' and thus 'emotion' element. So far we have discussed importance of management of emotions for business success and now we will proceed with discussing significance of emotional intelligence and the ways it should be used by business decision makers while making policies and strategies. Over the following sections we are going to discuss how five fortune 500 listed companies – Walmart, Tata Steel, British Petroleum, Toyota Motors and Samsung Electronics have made it to success by using emotional intelligence as the tool of their competitive advantage.

We are going to discuss managing EI with entrepreneur perspective, shareholder and investor perspectives, customer perspective, employee perspective, and society and environment perspective. Under each section, we will explain how from the perspective of each type of stakeholder, selected fortune 500 companies have implemented strategies and have earned great fortunes.

The Entrepreneur Perspective

Entrepreneur - an owner, founder, CEO or key manager of the business is a central role that influences behavior and performance of all other stakeholders in business. He is the one who is an important decision making authority and on the basis of these decisions other stakeholders perform their tasks. Although in big business setups it is impossible for entrepreneurs to interact with each and every stakeholder, they should be aware of interests and motives of all other stakeholders so that their decisions will be rightly synchronized with motives of associated group of people. No business can achieve success until and unless it ensures well alignment of top management goals with motives of other people involved directly or indirectly in business.

Entrepreneurs basically operate at top level of management and keep authority to manage and control lower levels of management. They make corporate strategies regarding all functional areas of business and keep 'people' in focus while doing that. Here 'people' does not only mean employees but people as all the respective stakeholders of business. Entrepreneurs are liable to take long term strategic decisions keeping business vision in mind. Business future course of planned functioning is stated by vision or mission statement or sometimes introduction, purpose or company's philosophy which it communicates to society.

Top management takes decisions in number of strategic areas. One of the key decisions is to develop right vision and mission of the company. Some companies have vision statement only, some have mission too, some have corporate value statement consisting both vision and mission, all have different ways to spell out their business philosophy in different manners. Fundamentally, vision and mission are the catalysts of business actions to be taken to achieve desired goals. Where vision deals with how company sees itself to be in future, mission statement clarifies how company will function to achieve what is stated in its vision statement.

Tata Steel

The Tata Steel, one of the Fortune 500 global companies has grown into one of the topmost global brands with special emphasis on human welfare.

Established in 1907, Tata Steel is among the top ten global steel companies with an annual crude steel capacity of over 28 million tonnes per annum (mtpa). It is now one of the world's most geographically-diversified steel producers, with operations in 26 countries and a commercial presence in over 50 countries.

Tata Steel's larger production facilities include those in India, the UK, the Netherlands, Thailand, Singapore, China and Australia. Operating companies within the Group include Tata Steel Limited (India), Tata Steel Europe Limited (formerly Corus), NatSteel, and Tata Steel Thailand (formerly Millennium Steel).[9]

Let us now have a look over mission statement of Tata Steel in which very first two lines, spell clearly company's commitment toward strengthening industrial base of the nation through effective utilization of staff and materials. Mission states that company recognizes that while honesty and integrity are the essential ingredients of a strong and stable enterprise, profitability provides the main spark for economic activity. Overall, the Company seeks to scale the heights of excellence in all that it does in an atmosphere free from fear, and thereby reaffirms its faith in democratic values.[10]

Tata Steel's Values include:

1. Respect for individuals
2. Integrity
3. Credibility
4. Trusteeship
5. Excellence

The primary value focuses upon 'respect for individuals' and sounds catchy as lot of emotional influence it exerts. Respect is a reward and every individual wants to be respected in all sort of personal and professional dealings. When a company like Tata Steel talks about respect for individuals, it gives great sense of emotional blessedness. Giving respect is not only that company talks about, but Tata has proven this too by adopting number of practices with different people segments and in various situations. Be it group of women, children, youth or elderly, Tata has been taking number of initiatives for the welfare of each group of Indian community. Company has been working for upgradation of these neglected groups by providing them with the means of basic livelihood, education and self dependence which finally can boost up sense of self respect amongst them. Tata thus, is known to really have deep emotions for individual's respect and gives good sense of emotional attachment of company to these people.

Use of word integrity in values shows Tata's concern and honesty towards business practices aligned with that of society's interests and wellbeing. Since ages this company is dedicated to the upliftment of underprivileged people in the country. Tata is known to serve society with continuous business growth and has sustained to be on list of most successful companies in the world. It is Tata's strategy to establish a 'society concerned' image which somewhere is contributing it back to achieve great competitive advantage.

Credibility word shows company's capacity of being capable to serve needs of concerned segments of market and society. Company's products are all manufactured keeping in view customer's value for their money and value of satisfaction they are going to derive by purchase of Tata products. This is how they have justified themselves as being 'trustee' of customer's money and their expectations by providing those best products and maximum value for money they spent. Over time Tata, as a group of brands has proved to be the supplier of best quality products in markets. Be it brand of salt, steel, motors, agrico, or telecommunications, Tata is considered to be the most trustworthy group of companies in India. Excellence is another value Tata promises to upkeep. Excellence in terms of productions, excellence in terms of social and environment protection, excellence in quality, excellence in quantity, excellence in employee satisfaction, excellence in customer satisfaction and excellence in all the areas of business and welfare activities. Excellence is something Tata has always ensured. It is Tata's core beliefs and emotionally established values that have taken company to the great heights of success.

Walmart

Walmart as per fortune 500 global companies list stands on topmost positions (No. 1 in 2011, No. 3 in 2012 and No. 2 in 2013). Being one of the topmost in terms of revenues, company has customer value as its focal point. Satisfaction of customers by providing them with great quality products and least possible price is company's primary concern. In previous section we have discussed the emotional intelligent vision of Sam Walton that envisaged Walmart's long term success and made it most successful retail company in world.

Sam Walton has devised magnificent strategy focused on almost all segments of market. His vision spelled in Walmart goals has been carried forward by Walmart management till date. In their purpose they specified that for them it is important to help people save their money so that they can live life better way. For a human being this concern captures great importance that a business firm, a retail store is concerned about their finances and savings and even trying to make their life better. Primarily in their purpose statement, they talk of promise to families about their concern for their well being. Word 'family' is always attached to human emotions strongest way. Even in individualistic communities, family depicts a happier association of people in relation. Walmart also focuses on fulfilling almost all product needs of consumers by making huge variety of products available inside one store. Continuously focusing on savings they talk about their initiatives, other measures of savings than just saving money in shopping. They are envisioning of introducing to their customers most energy efficient products with the use of which they can save more of their money. They target all local communities and supply products which suit their lifestyle.[11]

Number of statements as part of their mission is strongly emotionally structured and exhibit how people in different stages of their lives enjoy money they have saved in life. Sometimes by giving gift to grand children or cherishing ownership of very first home, it is their savings which drive their happiness. And finally it is Walmart which help them save maximum of their money.

If you see walmart purpose spelled clearly on its website you will find each word of depicts its concern for people well being, savings, choices, future, families, communities, lifestyle and moments. The perfectly emotionally established purpose plays pivotal role in Walmart's strategy to create the image of stakeholder centric store which helps it to achieve long term success and sustainable growth.

British Petroleum

Let us now throw light on how entrepreneurs at British Petroleum use emotional intelligence principles to carve out their fundamental goals and purpose. British Petroleum is UK based, one of the world's leading international oil and gas companies and is ranked sixth in fortune 500 list of most successful global companies for the year 2013. It provides its customers with fuel for transportation, energy for heat and light, retail services and petrochemicals products for everyday items.

Introducing themselves they say:

On British Petroleum website they have mentioned…

*"**We care deeply about how we deliver energy to the world.** Above everything, that starts with safety and excellence in our operations. This is fundamental to our success. Our approach is built on respect, being consistent and having the courage to do the right thing. We believe success comes from the energy of our people. We have a determination to learn and to do things better. We depend upon developing and deploying the best technology, and building long-lasting relationships. We are committed to making a real difference in providing the energy the world needs today, and in the changing world of tomorrow. We work as one team. We are BP."*[12]

In the beginning of the paragraph they exhibit their worldwide image and scope of operation whereby they demonstrate themselves to be the company which delivers energy to the 'World'. World they say is their market and capacity to serve such a huge segment finally ensures excellence of corporation that has made it worldwide successful concern. It says it finds resources, and produces various energy based products that are needed by people everywhere in the world. They also emphasize upon growing need of energy products for people and even for nations to grow. Growth is something that is highly needed by almost every person, entity and even by every nation in different terms. Further lines focus on company's intent to held high standards in whatever they do. To the great extent they have justified these lines in reality. BP despite of functioning in industry which is supposed to have highest risk, performs much efficiently due to its stress upon maintaining high standards in almost all areas of its operations right from finding the resources, their production, distribution, sale to after sale protocols.

They commit to be leaders of safety, world class operators, good corporate citizen and great employer. This commitment targets emotions of employees, investors and consumers when it talks of being great employer, safety leader and world class operators. Similarly, it targets emotions of masses in society when it calls itself a great corporate citizen.

Company also talks about what it stands for. It says its success lies in their care about how they deliver energy to the world, safety they ensure and excellence they thrive for. In order to stimulating emotions more they claim to have respect for all who are associated with BP by being consistent and righteous. They believe their success is outcome of the energy and efforts of its employees. They are learners, developers and deployers of best technology. They establish and maintain relationships, they are makers of tomorrow, catalysts of change, and entire BP works as a team. Each word spurs the emotions of readers by creating outstanding image of BP.

Company promises to have five values which finely translate its purpose.[13] The first and foremost value is 'safety' whereby they show their emotional concern for their employees, surrounded communities and environment. Second value enunciates 'respect' to entire world as company operates in the global environment. It ensures to work in compliance of all legal regulation. Fair and ethical image further strengthen while assuring to earn trust of others. 'Trust' another emotion stimulating factor exerts soothing impact. When we plan our purchase, the element of trust always induces us to buy the BP product as we all require products that are trustworthy. Further, they influence huge range of stakeholders and people they work with by showing their dependence on relationships they keep with all of them. Relationship and respect the emotional drivers motivate people from diverse groups, in varied nations to work for and with British Petroleum.

Here comes value to trigger emotions of customers - 'Excellence'. Company exhibits to operate with excellence through systematic and disciplined management. It works in accordance with rules and standards it has set for itself to confirm quality of its products. It emphasizes on constant learning for continuous improvement in right decision making. BP shows itself to have high 'Courage' as really it is involved in business which is full of uncertainties and requires die hard efforts of repeated nature. Still they are ready to speak up and stand by what they do and believe as they always do right things. Emotionally we all believe that courage comes from righteousness. One who does all right things has courage to speak up and stand by for all his decisions and doings. BP asks for help if it thinks it requires. Another quality portrayed is 'honesty', another emotional driver that pushes them to give them feedback of their operations. They desire to eternalize their legacy of wisdom, trust, courage, respect, trustworthiness, relationships, safety and respect despite having short term priorities like profits and revenues lined up.

Finally, BP attracts employees emphasizing their intent to work in teams. Human being emotionally is made to work in groups. In all communities, group work and effort is said to be the most effective approach to derive most effective outcome. Team is a formal task based group of people, an association wherein each individual with his motives and goals work in harmony with other members of the team for common purpose. Team work gives strong sense of association, the perfect organizational climate and culture where work is performed with high level of synchronization and efficiency of individuals in teams. Teams have their own climate of trust and of understanding. More the trust, easier it becomes to build up necessary competencies and capabilities in the organization. BP states that by trusting in each other and by keeping teams ahead of personal achievements, they acquire results expected out of their respective obligations.

British Petroleum has defined itself, its values in highly intellectual manner. It does not target only one group of people or groups but rather covers entire world as its area of operation. When it speaks about it concerns to serve the world with special focus on safety, respect, excellence, courage it basically envelopes almost all stakeholders associated with them. Consumers, employees, investors and society, emotions of all these parties have better been taken care in whatever they communicate to society.

Samsung Electronics

Samsung Electronics another fortune 500 company follows same philosophy of targeting emotions of people but in different way. Entrepreneurs at Samsung believe in future and communicate to society what they exactly are and want to continue with strong vision, philosophy and values.

Samsung in its vision seems to be future oriented and it is where it makes difference. Continuous success of decades is not sufficient for satisfaction and company needs to grow more. It wants to become one of the world's first five companies. This shows company's urging to lead the world by efficiency in all its operations and management. Samsung's slogan "Inspire the World, Create the Future" itself is quite self explanatory when we talk about emotional intelligent perspective of corporations. Samsung believes in creating future by inspiring people, people will include again all stakeholders with special emphasis upon customers of the company. Company believes in networking philosophy wherein they establish network with industry, partners and employees. Further they talk about their concern for employing highly talented workforce, giving them sufficient resources and facilities and getting best out of them in manufacturing products of superior quality.[14]

In order to execute its values Samsung has established five basic principles, stating what they do:[15]

1. Comply with laws and ethical standards
2. Maintain a clean organizational culture
3. Respect customers, shareholders and employees
4. Care for environment, health and safety
5. Socially responsible corporate citizenship

In its underlying principles, Samsung talks about its concern to adhere to all the laws and ethical standards, respect to customers and shareholders, care for environment, health and safety. They say they are socially responsible corporate citizens who maintain clean organizational culture. Governments, customers, shareholders, employees all are given a sensible touch of emotional consideration in Samsung set of principles and this is how entrepreneurs in Samsung make it to sustain strong position in global market arena.

Toyota Motors

Toyota is another example of world's most successful concerns that have proved their efficiency in managing sustainable growth over time. Toyota Motors secured eighth rank in the Fortune list of Global 500 companies for the year 2013. Toyota's guiding principles give clear understanding of its values and concern for emotions of its various stakeholders. The very first principle is – 'Honor the language and spirit of the law of every nation and undertake open and fair business activities to be a good corporate citizen of the world.'[16] Being global company it is very much important to ensure to the world that entering boundaries of other nations, company will not harm the existing environment of the other country. Language is an important part of the cultural system of every nation. People exchange their views and notions through language, which the medium to share thoughts, experiences and demands too. One's own language gives him the feeling of oneness and comfort. Further, legal system and laws vary from country to country depending upon overall system of society and administration concerns of the economy. Toyota keeping in mind these two important emotional aspects, language and laws tries to show itself being concerned to respect targeted market's social and community systems.

Another principle states that Toyota respects the culture and customs of every nation and contributes to economic and social development through corporate activities in the respective communities they enter worldwide. They also claim to dedicate their business to providing clean and safe products and to enhancing the quality of life everywhere through all of their activities. Respect for culture, customs, contribution to overall economic and social development, enhancement of quality of life each aspect exhibits the Toyota's vision inclined towards achieving global attention by stimulating emotions of different social units. Other statements in guiding principles signify Toyota's urge to create and develop advanced technologies and provide outstanding products and services that fulfill the needs of customers worldwide, foster a corporate culture that enhances both individual creativity and the value of teamwork while honoring mutual trust and respect between labor and management, pursue growth through harmony with the global community via innovative management, and work with business partners in research and manufacture to achieve stable, long-term growth and mutual benefits, while keeping themselves open to new partnerships. Each and every stakeholder in Toyota's portfolio is being targeted through guiding principles statements. Anyone belong to any group of stakeholders, may it be governments, shareholders, customers, partners, employees or even research communities worldwide would get great, affirmative impulse after going through these statements. Driven by their emotions it is quite obvious for all stakeholders to respond to company in the most positive way.

After discussing entrepreneurial perspectives with regard to emotional intelligence use in creating appealing vision, mission and value statements let us now talk about what these entrepreneurs, companies thrive to contribute to other stakeholders to create a socially responsible image of the concern and earn long run profits. In this light let us first discuss efforts of companies in - The Society and Environment Perspective

The Society and Environment Perspective

In newspapers, annual and sustainability reports, TV/Internet news and articles we usually come across news as to how 'big corporations' contribute to help societies grow and solve issues relative to their living, empowerment, environment protection etc. These types of strategies are formulated by companies to communicate to society that 'we care'. Society in general consists of business stakeholders, investors/shareholders, employees, government authorities, customers, suppliers, distributors and even environment at large. Companies by contributing to society, communities and environment contribute to well being of big array of even their indirect stakeholders.

Tata Steel

Tata's 'giving back to society' view helped Tata create a worldwide positive image and encouraged other corporations too to contribute back to society. Tata Council is the nodal agency of Tata group which specially looks after all the CSR activities including biodiversity issues, social empowerment, upliftment and development etc. and around 10400 Tata volunteers are working to contribute to welfare of society across India.

"The wealth gathered by Jamsetji Tata and his sons in half a century of industrial pioneering formed but a minute fraction of the amount by which they enriched the nation. The whole of that wealth is held in trust for the people and used exclusively for their benefit. The cycle is thus complete; what came from the people has gone back to the people many times over."[17]

- J.R.D. Tata

Tata has made remarkable contribution in social welfare initiatives. Number of upliftment drives for rural and underprivileged people has been leveraged by company included initiatives for social, economical and environmental development of rural areas, family planning and welfare programs, health awareness and prevention of acute diseases like leprosy, education, upliftment of scheduled tribes, women empowerment etc.

Tata Steel is committed to address problems arising due to climate change both by reducing its own carbon footprint and by creating high-performance steels that will make it possible to produce lighter, more fuel-efficient vehicles and energy-efficient buildings.

Company has already halved the amount of energy needed to make one tonne of steel over the last 40 years and has set itself a target of reducing CO_2 emissions by a further 20% within the next decade.[18]

Tata Steel is highly focused on Tata's values and mission which emphasize on achieving excel through societal development. These 'human' based emotional values of Tata forces one to opt for Tata products having in mind Tata's concrete image of human concern. Emphasizing on society Tata emphasizes also on establishing and sustaining its favorable reputation in the eyes of all its stakeholders.

Walmart

As discussed earlier, initiatives companies adopt for social and environmental well being are sort of emotional intelligence tactics that help them sustain the favorable image amongst its stakeholders. Walmart proudly says that it contributes to society by number of initiatives like - Giving, Women Empowerment, Renewable Energy, Hunger Relief and Diversity

Save Money. Live Better! Walmart says they live by these words and the work they do to help people live better goes beyond their store walls. Supporting organizations that positively impact local communities around the globe is something they consider part of their mission. According to Walmart 2013 Global Responsibility Report, their total cash giving of that year is more than $311 including $273 US cash and $38 as international cash. Walmart, Sam's Club and Logistics associates volunteered more than 2.2 million hours, generating $18 million for local U.S. nonprofits. Walmart also contributed $3.8 million in cash and in-kind support to those impacted by disasters across the U.S.[19]

Report also says that to date Walmart Foundation has trained nearly 17000 women in India and Bangladesh. They also encourage other retailer brands and suppliers to replicate the program, have collaborative partnerships to contribute to women empowerment. Walmart had launched the Global Women's Economic Empowerment Initiative in the year 2011 and by using their great size, scale and commitment to human welfare they are empowering women across the world

Walmart is also committed to contribute to environment protection and is confirmed as largest on site green power generator in the United States by EPA green power partnership and is also recognized by the Solar Energy Industries Association (SEIA) as having the most installed on-site solar capacity in the U.S. Moreover, company has received the Renewable Energy Leader of the Decade award from the American Council on Renewable Energy (ACORE).[20]

According to the data available from the U.S. Department of Agriculture, at some point in 2011, more than 50 million people in the U.S. struggled with hunger. Of that number, more than 16 million were children. Walmart and the Walmart Foundation took up this is a big issue and, as the world's largest grocer, they were in good position to help. Walmart collaborated with organizations such as Feeding America and Share Our Strength, and leveraged their size and

> *"On behalf of the 37 million clients of Feeding America and our national network of food banks, I'd like to thank Walmart and its associates for helping us fight hunger together in our communities. The 1 billion meals you've donated to our network have helped bring nutritious food to families across the country. We're grateful for your partnership and look forward to working side-by-side with you and your associates as we continue to feed those in need."*
>
> - Bob Aiken, president and CEO, Feeding America

Source: Walmart, 2013 Global Responsibility Report, Available at: http://az204679.vo.msecnd.net/media/documents/updated-2013-global-responsibility-report_130113953638624649.pdf accessed on 6/7/13

scale to provide nutritious food and resources to help society fight this serious issue. Walmart Foundation under Walmart's Hunger Relief initiative with association of other partners surpassed 1 billion meals donated.[21]

Just have a look over what Bob Aiken has mentioned about Walmart. The way Bob has expressed his gratitude to his associates inspires great sense of actualization amongst those who contributed to this purpose. Also when readers read this as the part of Walmart 2013 Global Responsibility Report, their respect and dignity grows higher and higher for Walmart and make them feel proud if they are direct stakeholders of this company.

British Petroleum

BP talks about its contribution to society in its vision and purpose statements which we discussed in the earlier sections. Their activities generate jobs, investment, infrastructure and revenues for governments and local communities.

They believe that innovative technology and strong relationships with governments, partners and communities around the world underpin their activities. They are working with state and federal trustee agencies to evaluate injury to natural resources and are supporting long-term research into the potential impacts of oil spills on ecosystems. BP has funded several different types of restoration projects. According to BP Sustainability Review 2012, BP has started working on restoration project, expected to cost approximately $60 million, aimed to collectively restore and enhance wildlife, habitats, the ecosystem services provided by those habitats, and provide additional access for fishing, boating and related recreational uses. BP annually reviews its management of material issues such as greenhouse gas, water, and sensitive and protected areas.[22]

Being member of the World Ocean Council, an international, cross-sector alliance for industry leadership and collaboration, BP is working to further their understanding of sustainable practices in marine environments and develop approaches to resource management and planning that balance the needs of industry, recreation and conservation. At the onset of new projects, BP assesses what might be the short and long term impacts would these projects have over environment. They do the early screening; assess number of factors including the needs of indigenous people, human rights implications, security, community needs, workforce welfare and local employment, the cultural heritage of the area, and the physical and economic aspects of involuntary resettlement.[23] Further, BP engages in number of other social and environmental protection initiatives like community investment, education, lobbying, advocacy, anti bribery, corruption etc. which help BP to create and sustain most socially responsible corporation image in the society.

Samsung Electronics

In 2012 sustainability report, Samsung mentions that in order to contribute to societies, they engage in a variety of activities for local communities such as support programs for children, teen education, medical benefits for low-income families and their global social contribution initiative, 'the Samsung Hope for Children'. Under their environmental responsibility Samsung has announced the the "Eco-Management 2013" initiative as per which they promoted various environmental programs such as the reduction of greenhouse gas emissions and the development of eco-friendly products. Samsung being highly innovative in research have invented a variety of eco-friendly, high performance products with ultra low-power memory chips which greatly reduces energy consumption due to the improved energy efficiency. Four Samsung products including the world's first solar-charging laptop, a microwave oven, a laundry machine and transparent LCDs, received Eco Design awards at the Consumer Electronics Show (CES) 2012. Also Samsung has been recognized as 'Energy Star Partner of the Year' by the U.S. Environmental Protection Agency (EPA) for two consecutive years and named as one of 100 green foreign companies in China by China Europe International Business School (CEBIS).[24]

Samsung Electronics has developed water policies to have enhanced stakeholder communication and minimization of management risk. In 2011, Samsung Electronics and its subsidiaries contributed KRW (Korean Won) 293.7 billion to local communities. In Korea, they donated KRW 30.1 billion for arts and culture, KRW 27.8 billion for personal development, and KRW 95.8 billion for social welfare programs as well as KRW 4.5 billion for other activities including it hearing dogs program for the hearing impaired. KRW 34.9 billion was given, outside Korea to such projects as IT education for developing regions and donations to the Amazon Environmental Foundation. Moreover, company fosters passionate culture of volunteering as 288,586 employees donated their time in volunteering in the year 2011. [25]

Toyota Motors

In order to contribute to the sustainable and harmonious societal development, Toyota Motor Corporation and its subsidiaries have constantly been taken number of initiatives in almost all regions company is functional. These initiatives are driven by Toyota guiding principles. They seek to protect environment by minimizing impact of their own business operations. They are focused on producing vehicles that do not affect climate and biodiversity in a harmful manner. Under guiding principle 3, They seek to develop and promote technologies that enable economies and environment to coexist harmoniously and by developing strong relationships with organizations and individuals who support them in their mission of preserving environment. According to their guiding principle 2, "respect for people" they implement value to honor all cultures, history, customs and laws of all the nations. Company does not tolerate bribery in any of its dealing and adhere to maintain all relationships with high levels of integrity and honesty as per their guiding principle 1. Under their social contribution activities, Toyota works individually and with its partners to strengthen the enrichment of the society with number of initiatives[26]

The Shareholder and Investor Perspective

Finance is always considered as the lifeblood of business and investors and shareholders are providers of this important resource. But what does it take to attract these parties to invest in your business? It is reward. Reward in form of share in profits, dividends is the great motivator for investors and shareholders. Companies that provide higher returns on shareholders investment find it easy to attract more and more investment for further functioning and expansion projects. Money, as a matter of fact is not considered as a very strong motivator as it is perceived to create only the time bound, extrinsic motivation, number of researches has proved that money has got great significance with respect to person's overall life satisfaction. It is money dearth of which put people in state of depression and high levels of mental distress. On the contrary people with sound financial background enjoy their lives better ways. Happiness and contentment, these two fundamental emotions are directly linked with money. More money buys more materials that give emotional happiness and satisfaction to the human being and thus when investors receive good returns on their investments (money) they get more motivated to invest in the specific business or corporation. Fortune 500 companies are those companies whose sustainability is high, who generate maximum revenues and profits and finally who give back their investors best returns and rewards out of their investments. Let us have a look now how our companies give their investors the perfect emotional motivation to invest more in their shares.

Tata Steel

Tata Steel shareholders enjoy high degree of emotional satisfaction, deep sense of security and pride. Through the years shareholders have helped company to venture to great expansion and globalization and therefore Tata is committed to enhance shareholder value even during the times when company profits are not very high. Company's communication strategy with its investors has evolved from simple written documents to highly interactive online reports. Tata has established, nurtured and flourished the relationship that is based upon transparency, governance and trust.[27]

Tata Steel – the brand has been recognized as the symbol of trust across India and also the countries where it functions. The company's slogan 'Values stronger than steel' inspires great level of trust amongst all stakeholders of the company. Tata is also

> "Despite the weakening market conditions in the last year, the Indian operations posted a strong growth in production and deliveries. Our investment over the years in customer relationship building, developing distribution chain, undertaking market research and retail focus paid dividend through the significant sequential increase in deliveries in the last quarter. I convey my heartiest congratulations to all the employees for achieving this commendable performance. The brownfield expansion is now fully ramped up and we are committed to commissioning the greenfield plant in Odisha on schedule. The South East Asian operations have performed well with improving demand, product differentiation, efficiency improvement and restructuring measures."
>
> Tata Steel Managing Director
> Mr HM Nerurkar

Source: Tata 2013 Tata Steel Group reports Consolidated Financial Results for the Financial Year ended March 31, 2013, available at:http:// www.tatasteelindia.com/usernewsroom/viewfile.asp ?filename=WhatNew_2013_5_23_26_42_968.pdf

known as the company which has registered most desirable sustainable growth even in times of worldwide recession. Despite bearing losses in Europe in recession, company is again on its way to recover the damages to protect its investors from any financial losses. Tata's great concern to protect its investors and shareholders has influenced investors across the globe and this is the reason why Tata is able to ensure such smooth sustainable growth in the market.

Walmart

Walmart has great history of delivering strong financial results with its well planned and effectively implemented strategies. When it comes to investors and shareholders, Walmart ensures them with most positive, constant and guaranteed returns. Rob Walton, Chairman of the Board of Directors, Walmart states: "We are guided by strong governance principles in our service to shareholders, and in making decisions that strengthen our ability to serve customers,"[28]

Walmart emphasize lot upon managing its governance structure location to location and store to store. Corporation is governed by well experienced Chairman and highest quality Board of Directors who help organization to serve its investors with global compliance standards. Company directors with diversity of thoughts, are recognized leaders in their fields, each with experience and expertise covering many global industries – retail, technology, finance, brand management, and strategy. This diversity of perspective is critical to providing guidance to management and this strong guidance is reflected in company's financial results.

Walmart President and Chief Executive Officer Mike Duke in his letter to shareholders states, "I'm pleased with our business and financial performance last year (2012). But what gives me the most confidence is the changing landscape of retail around the world, and how our people, our strategies and the customers we know and care about fit in. Whether it's everyday low prices, a seamless shopping experience, the most talented team of associates or our model for making a difference, we are on the right path."[29]

Over the last decade, Walmart has reported to grew sales by approximately 7 percent on a compounded annual rate, earnings per share by approximately 11 percent on a compounded annual rate, and returned close to $100 billion to shareholders in the form of dividends and share repurchases. Walmart is continuing even in fiscal year 2013, its long history of delivering strongest results and great value to its shareholders. Company has been performing consistent and strong, even during times when the global economy was volatile.

Walmart bases its strategies on its financial priorities – growth, leverage and returns and this is how it has continued to create great value for itself and for its shareholders.[30]

Walmart considers 'delivering strong returns to shareholders' as it top priority and its AA credit rating is a proof of Walmart's strong cash flows, disciplined financial management and the strength of their underlying business due to which they are able to invest more in company's growth and ensure high returns to shareholders both through dividends and share repurchases. Walmart's annual dividend per share has increased about 18 percent on average over the last decade, and they have returned over $60 billion in share repurchases and dividends over the last five years alone.[31] And this is the reason why Walmart shareholders are emotionally inclined toward investing in Walmart and are contributing to company's leverage ensuring long term sustainable growth.

British Petroleum

BP aims to create value for shareholders by helping society meet growing demand for energy in a responsible manner. Engaging with shareholders and investors, communicating with them often, help BP to make most appropriate decisions. They interact with shareholders and analysts through their annual general meeting and other events. They communicate via roadshows, webcasts and one-to-one meetings. In 2012, this included a presentation on BP Energy Outlook 2030, and briefings on oil sands and their progress against safety enhancements.

BP is expert in establishing the most powerful corporate image in investor's minds by its rigorous efforts to sustain that image over time. BP is always ready and well placed to handle all unsettled conditions, turbulence, political upheavals and unexpected crisis. Its global footprint and prudent financial approach help it to sustain its growth in smooth manner. According to Bob Dudley, Group Chief Executive in BP Annual Report and Form 20-F 2012, in shaping BP's portfolio, they are prioritizing shareholder value in a consistent way. For BP, scale always remains important, but they are now more focused on driving forward their financial performance rather than simply growing production volumes. They expect that operating cash flow and replacement cost profit will take precedence over barrels of production. To provide investors with strongest returns, they are increasing investment in the areas with the greatest potential to generate strong and reliable growth in operating cash flow, from exploration and deepwater operations to giant fields and gas value chains. In the Downstream, they have a portfolio of world-class businesses that are positioned to deliver material and growing free cash flows. During the year 2012, they gained new access in six countries. Since 2010 they have accessed around 400,000 square kilometres of new acreage. That is roughly the size of California and more than double the exploration acreage gained from 2000 to 2009.[32]

Apart from being the company that ensures great returns to its shareholders, with its great expansion BP has established itself with the top notch image of a huge corporation with differentiated products and diverse portfolio. Investors and shareholders feel it matter of pride to invest in such an elite class company which continues to have an important presence in many of the world's largest economies and in fast-developing countries.

Samsung Electronics

Despite completion getting more intense, in the year 2012, Samsung recorded the historic sales revenue and operating profit enhancing shareholders and investors returns and Samsung's leadership position in the global electronics market. Based on consolidated financial statements, Samsung realized sales revenue of KRW 201 trillion, operating profit of KRW 29 trillion and net income of KRW 24 trillion, double the previous year. They also maintained a robust financial structure, with a 49.1 percent liability ratio and 79.5 percent capital adequacy rato.[33]

Samsung investors get fascinated by Samsung's market leadership with most innovative product strategies. Samsung Electronics has been expanding its market leadership in its core businesses, including smartphones and TVs. In both their mobile phone and television business they have been sustaining No. 1 with respect to market share

> *"The power to keep growing is directly fueled by the trust and dedication of our customers, shareholders and society. Looking ahead in 2013, Samsung Electronics will continue to work toward the change and innovation that inspires the world and shapes new futures."*
>
> Oh-Hyun Kwon
> Vice Chairman & CEO,
> Samsung Electronics

Source: 2012 Samsung Electronics Annual Report
http://www.samsung.com/us/ aboutsamsung/investor_relations/ financial_information/downloads/2013/ SECAR2012_Eng_Final.pdf

and profitability. With its newly reorganized structure of three divisions, company is expected to aggressively respond to rapidly changing business environments as it has now started to steer new technology initiatives, pioneer new markets and identify new business opportunities across the globe.

Further, Samsung has established strong brand name by winning number of laurels that keep investors attracted to invest in Samsung. Its differentiated capabilities and technology earned worldwide recognition, including four awards from the European Imaging and Sound Association 2012 (EISA), the most prestigious in the region's video and audio industry, and 27 innovation awards at CES 2013, the world's largest consumer electronics show. They also advanced high profile and consistent global brand marketing by sponsoring a range of international sports events, including the London 2012 Summer Olympics. As a result of such efforts, they attained the No. 9 ranking on Interbrand's Best 100 Global Brands 2012 list, with an estimated brand value of USD 32.9 billion.[34]

Toyota Motors

Basic management principles of Toyota include Toyota's concern to contribute to society while also focusing on long term company growth. Toyota believes that it is important to devise financial policies focused on three key components viz. 'growth', 'efficiency' and 'stability' as by doing that it is more likely to achieve long term sustainable growth by maintaining its great corporate value. Toyota investors and shareholders enjoy great returns as Toyota always aims to sustain its growth by focusing on manufacturing better cars even in most turbulent market environments. Customers give high preference to Toyota vehicles by purchasing its cars and enabling company to invest more in better manufacturing. Their global vision of sustainability along with enrichment of the lives of the community is helping them to achieve greater profits. Even during the harsh economic environment with a yen/dollar exchange rate of ¥85 to the dollar and a unit sales volume of 7.5 million cars, they ensure to venture to restore Toyota (unconsolidated) to profitability. Toyota is expecting to work toward achieving a consistent consolidated operating income of approximately one trillion yen and a consolidated operating income ratio of 5%.[35]

Great instance of Toyota's struggle towards achieving its vision is when in 2011, Production was reduced due to great East Japan earthquake and the floods in Thailand, Toyota managed to normalize the production more than expected speed and restored production with high devotion in its concern toward sustainability of the corporation. Entire group joined together to cut the costs and counter the effects of sharp appreciation of the yen and accomplished better constitutional improvement to create more solid profitability.[36]

Toyota's aim of 'making ever better cars' captures investor's attention to Toyota's concern for excellence in car manufacturing. In its 2012 Annual Report, Toyota mentions that they are now focusing on revitalizing their venture spirit by their efforts such as joint ventures with other corporations followed by their global vision. They are targeting to invigorate areas of development, procurement and design. Also company is much more concerned to strengthen supply chains to minimize parts procurement risk. As far as production area is concerned Toyota is restoring their 'Monozukuri' (conscientious manufacturing) structure as the basis for production technology and structure innovation. They are expecting 40% to 50% increase in global sales made up by emerging markets by introducing cars that meet local needs of people in different communities and sections of the society.[37]

The Customer Perspective

Business entities survive by fulfilling demand of products and services by respective customers in the market. And in today's highly dynamic business environment, customer loyalty has become one of the most crucial tasks to manage and ensure. Due to availability of innumerable substitutes of almost every product, customer can easily switch to other options. It is human tendency that he wants the maximum satisfaction from each unit of money he spends on buying articles he needs and this is the reason why companies try to provide customers best value for their money. As a matter of fact in monopolistic and oligopoly market situations, there remains more pressure on producers as to how to differentiate their products from their competitors in order to enhance their sale over others. And this differentiation element should always be something unique that would emotionally attract customer to prefer that product. Further, relationship that companies establish and sustain with customers also affects the customer lifetime value and brand loyalty. In this section we are going to discuss how our fortune 500 companies have made it to earn fortunes by attracting their customers in a different yet similar manner.

Tata Steel

Tata Steel produces goods and services to meet standards and needs of the construction sector on global level. Tata Steel's range of materials, products and services, include: steel plate and sections, armoured steel, blast protective structures, perimeter security, anti-attack vehicle barriers, as well as engineering consultancy and solutions.[38] Tata Steel is always mindful of what customers exactly need. They regularly receive inputs from customers and then establish their strategic goals on emerging needs and future product applications. Tata Steel's New Product Development programme, knowledge-sharing and customer engagement initiatives are the great outcome of such practice. To illustrate this, we can talk about Tata's 'Steelovation' initiative which is designed to provide maximum value to the customers. It is basically targeted on key account customers of Galvano and Steelium brands and based upon their feedback, Tata Steel customize its products to enhance value to maximum and to ensure the end customer satisfactio.[39]

> *"This is the world in which Tata Steel seeks to excel, by providing the best quality products and the best possible service to our customers. The stated purpose is to create solutions to the ever changing needs, using the material that plays a vital role in all everyone's lives. Steel is exceptionally strong, durable and versatile, as well as being 100% recyclable. As a Fortune 500 company and one of the world's most geographically diversified steel producers, we are not only meeting the current needs of our global customer base but are also developing exciting new solutions in steel that will deliver additional value to our customers in the future."*

Source: Tata Steel – The world of steel brochure available at: http://www.tatasteel.com/media/pdf/group-brochure.pdf

Tata Steel Flat products launched the 'Steelovation' initiative to share the knowledge with customers. Having customer issues in the core the initiative focuses on getting actual feedback from customers to produce customized products that fit absolutely to consumer demand and expectations. Feedback, as part of this initiative is taken by highly interactive sessions where customers are encouraged to feel free to ask any questions they have for Tata Steel products and discuss issues they feel they have some. This helps Tata to enhance value of its products by ensuring the end customer satisfaction.[40]

Tata Steel is highly focused on enhancing customer satisfaction and strengthening relationships with its existing customers. Company has adopted several new initiatives striving to achieve better customer service in each market segment. In 2002, company implemented VTS (Vehicle Tracking System). Across the country, approx 1600 GPS (Global Positioning System) mounted vehicles were deployed making initiative the largest implementation of GPS enabled fleet in the steel industry. A billboard has been created and uploaded on specific webpage to track vehicles online with the motive to ensure and improve the reliability of delivery. In order to reduce service claims company developed infrastructure at various hubs and stock yards including specialized vehicles. Also, an auto complaint hub is developed in Chennai to create service differentiation and for receipt, storage, handling and delivery of steel materials and stock points, standard operating procedures have been implemented. Another commendable initiative is creation of transport parks in Jamshedpur to address the issues related to traffic flow, safety and health of drivers. Approximately 2000 drivers undergo medical checkup at Tata Steel facilities every month.[41] Tata focuses on strengthening its overall supply, distribution and logistics system to ensure its consumer the best service with maximum emotional satisfaction.

Walmart

Walmart claims that it is customers always with whom Walmart responsibility starts with. In today's world for governments, communities and for people in general, it is very difficult to face major issues and challenges posed by economic upheavals on global level. Walmart therefore thrives to contribute to solve most of the problems by its initiatives to provide best customer value by its huge global retail operations.

It was Sam Walton, founder of Walmart who cultivated customer focused culture in the corporation since its inception. In his autobiography "Sam Walton - Made in America: My Story," Walton stated ten rules that he followed in managing his company. One of the rules said, *"Exceed your customer's expectations. If you do they'll come back over and over. Give them what they want - and a little more. Let them know you appreciate them. Make good on all your mistakes, and don't make excuses - apologize. Stand behind everything you do. 'Satisfaction guaranteed' will make all the difference."* In 2002 Departmental Store Customer Satisfaction Study, Walmart was ranked number one by its customers reflecting Walton's vision of providing best service to customers.[42]

One of the example of Sam's customer oriented approach is the 'ten-foot rule' which ensures that a customer who passes within ten feet of an employee should be assisted in the most helpful and courteous manner. They also spend time in assessing and understanding customer needs and expectations. Following practices are adopted at Walmart to ensure efficient follow up of the ten foot rule:[43]

- Look at the customer in the eye
- Greet the customer
- Ask the customer if s/he needs any help.

Walmart constantly researches and modify its policies with respect to customer satisfaction. Its initiatives like low price every day attracts customers by giving them feel of 'saving their hard earned money' with Walmart. Not only in the USA, but Walmart is performing outstanding worldwide since decades due to its most emotional intelligent customer focused policies. Sam Walton, leader with high EQ, identified what in general would attract all customers irrespective of their different demographic backgrounds. It was less and best price as money is one thing which almost every customer value and wants best out of every unit of spending. After purchasing from Walmart, customer rest satisfied that he has spent right amount of money on his purchase and this emotional satisfaction brings him back to Walmart over and over again.

However, price is not the only feature that attracts customers toward Walmart stores. Company also offers branded and unbranded goods without compromise on quality standards of the products. Over and over in its advertisements and promotions Walmart repeat that it provides best value of customer's money by providing less priced high quality products. Walmart also has started to focus upon how to solve product availability and accessibility issues in different markets and locations. In order to make Walmart products more accessible, to reach to mass consumers and to have a direct interface with customers, Walmart has ventured into the e-business services. Best price, good quality and easy availability with innumerable more benefits, Walmart customers have helped Walmart to record great revenues making it the topmost retail store chain in the world.

British Petroleum

British Petroleum caters to almost all needs of consumers when it comes to their demands for petroleum products. Through their operations they provide customers with fuel for transportation, energy for heat and light, lubricants to keep engines moving, and the petrochemicals products used to make everyday items as diverse as paints, clothes and packaging. Their projects and operations help to generate employment, investment and tax revenues in countries and communities around the world helping them solve major economic problems.

At present BP is serving the major energy markets of the world. Focusing on safe and reliable value chains BP they are able to achieve the great competitive returns and sustainable growth. BP knows better how to use technology and research as effective tools to make difference. BP strongly focus on customer feedback which help them to know how well they are fulfilling their customer's expectations and what are the areas they need to further improve. For BP, criteria of customer satisfaction includes: product grades/specification, overall product availability, quality etc. Number of loyalty programs have been launched by BP to create unique value and help BP differentiate and becoming most preferable option for its customers. With its great emphasis over research and development, BP creates better market prospects. It is now producing gasoline that cleans the engine, increase mileage and help customer save their money.[44] Despite being criticized lot for its deepwater horizon case, BP did not give up. In order to rejuvenate its image, it took help of customer value propositions which are targeted to soothe customer's emotions. Offering emotion stimulating programs and conducting new marketing campaigns, BP has revamped its brand value and has used customer's emotions as the tool to sustain its market position.

Samsung Electronics

In order to provide maximum emotional satisfaction to customers, Samsung believe in making products that are reliable and ensure customer's safety and health. Company has undertaken several projects to acquire the international safety certification. Also number of other initiatives has been adopted at Samsung like applying methods to develop and sell the safest products. In their Manufacturing Execution System, Samsung has incorporated a reliability evaluation system to confirm to produce products that are highly reliable and guarantee the best performance. Continuing great emphasis on quality, company has also started to focus on other measures like stronger quality inspections, operate with taskforce team of experts etc.[45]

Along with focus on quality, Samsung has to offer electronic products suitable for all segments of market. To illustrate, Samsung mobile phones with great range have recorded grand success due to their good quality, reasonable price, brand name, unique and advanced features and much more that drives great emotional satisfaction amongst customers. Samsung has great capability to catch the customer's pulse. As a matter of fact company believes in seeing eye to eye with customers and listening what they have to say. They gather customer choice, preference, concern, and complaints related information through VOC – Voice of Customer surveys. In order to respond rapidly to customer complaints, concerns and queries, daily inspection meetings are held with customer response related departments like sales, development, quality, technology and production.[46]

Samsung believes in producing goods that are truly needed by customers. To assess this need again Samsung undertake the survey to know what customer expectations really are with respect to electronic goods. On the basis of the results then company develops the products, each time better products that meet customer's expectations. To minimize complaints and to maximize customer satisfaction is at the core of Samsung's value proposition that results in delivering great emotional value to the consumers of Samsung products.

Toyota Motors

For Toyota their greatest reward is the smiles they earn from their customers. Company gets involved in lot of research to identify expectations with respect to what gives them maximum emotional satisfaction. What is customer's definition of 'great cars'? are they already available in the market? How can Toyota produce 'great cars' for them and provide maximum emotional satisfaction ensuring strong customer lifetime value. They know that customer expectations in today's business scenario change constantly and to respond to such ever changing expectations, Toyota has developed the system to constantly listen to customer voice and work continually on improvement.[47]

Toyota believes that it is important to respond to customer's satisfaction and put 'Customer' and 'Quality' as their first and most important concern. With this purpose every Toyota employee takes responsibility and ownership to ensure high level customer satisfaction and customer loyalty. Toyota has integrated its former quality and customer service operations group to form a new 'Customer First Promotion Group' in the year 2012. This group is totally dedicated towards:[48]

- Integrating functions to handle quality issues in the service field closely involved with customers;
- Putting their customer first policy into practice;
- Implementing customer centered sales plans and operational development and
- Engaging in initiatives to strengthen support for dealers' service capabilities

Company has deployed the 'Toyota Advanced Quality Information Center (T-AQIC)' globally to ensure the early detection and early resolution of quality related issues in a rapid and smooth manner. Also, aiming to foster human resources focusing on quality, the principle of "Ji Kotei-Kanketsu (built-in quality with ownership)" was added to the global contents of level-specific education in January 2012. With the help of dealers and the Customer Assistance Centers, they obtain customer opinions to make better cars with superior features in terms of environmental, safety and quality performance while also offering the intrinsic appeal such as driving performance at an affordable price. Another initiative is the Customer Month, the month of May when entire month they make efforts to permeate their principle of customer first to provide customers with products and services that earn their true, emotionally satisfied smiles.[49]

Customer being in the nucleus of business strategies is considered to be the most important stakeholder of the business and fortune 500 companies know very well how to capture and manage better customer relationships. They put every possible effort to provide maximum satisfaction to ensure customer lifetime value. It is nothing but the game of emotions where businesses allure the customers by attracting their emotional response and then manage to have them connected with business by maintaining their emotional attraction towards the company.

The Employee Perspective

In business, human resource is considered as the fundamental resource that is used to get all work done focused on organizational goals and objectives. It is therefore most important to have this resource always engaged in a manner that it ensures higher level efficiency in terms of performance and productivity. In this part, we will first discuss the general significance of EI in life of an employee, considering employee as a 'human being' whose behavior and performance is completely driven by his emotions. Later in section, we are going to discuss how big companies make efforts to manage people using EI.

To live it perfect way everyone needs balance in life. Balance denotes sufficient satisfaction human being derive from his roles in all spheres of life. For most of the human beings there are two broad spheres of life - personal and professional. Both spheres are mutually dependent. Each sphere has various roles to be played. Slight imbalance in one role can create huge disturbance to all other roles person is supposed to play during course of his life. In various researches conducted across the world it is proved that most of the problems in organizations are 'people' and 'behavior' specific. Behavior which is nothing but an outcome of emotional processing of human brain is responsible for all positive and negative actions of human being. It is therefore important to understand that in order to ensure the positive and productive behavior it is necessary to manage emotions in most positive manner.

Strong emotional intelligence is the vital requirement to manage people around all spheres of human's life. In daily course of life you interact with number of people for your professional and non professional concerns. If you spend eight hours on your job at least four hours you spend in your non professional dealings. Family, friends, colleagues and even those with whom we interact in general like ones sitting in the market, vendors, grocers etc. are integral parts of our lives. Being human beings they also need to get managed emotional intelligent ways. Family relationships, prior concern for most of us can only be nurtured on strong emotional platform. It is perceived that employees having healthy and happy relationships at home are found to be more productive at their workplaces.

Happiness makes minds healthy. Happiness is source of energy and cure for most of the psychological problems, signifies the positivity and perfection of situations around the person. It comes from your inside, from your heart and your heart is directly attached with people you love, may be your spouse, children, parents siblings or friends. Slight disturbance with these relationships can spoil your mood for long time and this mental stress directly affects your work performance. Hence in order to be more productive it is not sufficient to practice your emotional expertise on your workplace only. You have to manage your personal relationships also with high levels of EI if you want to achieve overall balance in your life. Similarly in order to keep your personal life happy and satisfied, you need smooth professional life. Job with good rewards, motivation and satisfaction leaves positive impact on your personality and makes your personal life happy.

Person with high levels of emotional intelligence always thrives to achieve great balance between both professional and personal sides of his life which help him to perform most effective ways. His efficiency would be highly visible in well planned, organized and controlled tasks with perfect managerial abilities and high intrinsic motivation to achieve desired goals in his life.

From the side of employee, he needs to manage balance between personal and professional roles to ensure better efficiency in his performance. Now if we take employers into consideration they should also seek to help employees to manage this personal and professional life balance. They should provide employees with healthy work culture including elements of trust, mutual understanding, care, good reward system etc. to boost up sense of happiness in them. They should be careful enough to ensure that organizational efficiency should not get affected due to any setback in management of human resources or their emotions.

Employee Persona and the Game of Roles

Being human beings we play number of roles at a time. You play roles of father or mother, employee, son or daughter, sister or brother, friend, member of some club or association etc at the same time. People associated with each role have different types of expectations from you and you also have different expectations from your different roles. Figure 2 below shows the simple role map of an individual. Role map shows closeness of various roles of an individual to his 'self'. For example the role map in the figure belongs to Sue Carla and innermost circle of the map is her 'self'. The second inner circle is the role of a mother which is closest to her heart, most important relationship which gives her most intense happiness. Third circle is 'spouse' and she is highly concerned about responsibilities she needs to fulfill in this role due to beautiful emotional bond she is having with her husband. Fourth circle is her role as a daughter. She has wonderful parents who love her immensely and care lot about her. She is also strongly attached to them. She has got a younger sister who lives with her and is dependent completely on Sue for due to prolonged health problems of their old parents. This role of sister is fifth circle. Sue works with a multinational corporation as a marketing executive and she keeps this role on the sixth and the last position in her role map.

Sue's husband gets transferred to the other location and she needs to decide whether she would leave her job and move along with her husband? Or she will continue with her job and let her husband move alone to the new job location? Now, what will be the main factor that will affect her final decision? It would primarily be her level of emotional attachment with her husband and her job. She may decide to move considering she will not be able to survive without her husband or she may decide to continue to stay in existing location because she thinks she may not get such good job and great organization in the city her husband is shifting to. And what does 'great organization' means here? It is organization which has ability to emotionally connect with feeling of the employees by fulfilling all existential and emotional needs. Existential needs like needs for materials, food, clothes, shelter, comfort and luxury goods can be fulfilled by monetary rewards (like compensation, remuneration etc). On the other hand emotional needs like good work environment, relationships at workplace, job satisfaction, status and esteem, recognition and appreciation etc can be fulfilled by measures taken to elate motivation and morale without using power of money. For most of us primary reason why we choose to work is because we want to earn 'money'. We generate money from our jobs to fulfill existential needs but at the same time we have emotional needs too. In this way money is just a kind of motivator and does not drive complete motivation.

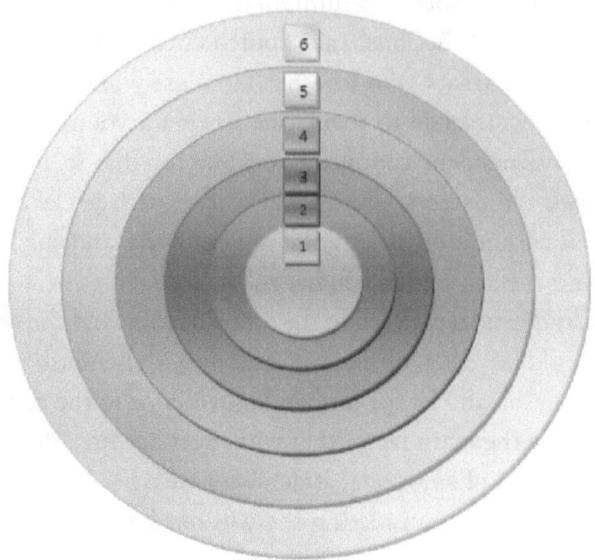

Figure 2 The Role Map

Organizations that manage emotions of employees well also become successful to place themselves closer to employee's self in employee's role map. This closeness to 'self' signifies employee's higher level of emotional attachment with the organization resulting in strong commitment, belongingness, low possibility of attrition and less absenteeism. Employees prefer to carry on to workplace where they receive both financial and emotional stability. This is why it is a challenging task before leaders and entrepreneurs to provide employees the ideal atmosphere to work which can ensure better emotional attachment of employees with the organization. Now let us see what our Fortune 500 corporations do to ensure strong emotional attachment of their employees to drive most efficient performance at workplaces.

Tata Steel

Talking about employees, Tata Steel considers its employees as main source of competitiveness. Group is committed toward number of strong strategies for human resource development. The strategies focus on clearly defining the job profile and responsibilities for the job and matching right person to job which help them to put right person on the right job. Another focal area confirms that all performance is appraised in a fair and transparent manner. Further, reward system of group ensures alongside monetary reward there should be adequate scope for non monetary rewards as promotions, delegation of authorities and responsibilities etc.

Tata Steel is the world's second most geographically diversified steel producer, employing around 80,000 people across five continents in nearly 50 countries. Tata Steel strives towards its vision to become the pioneer with respect to value creation and corporate citizenship with excellence of its employees, innovation and overall conduct. Tata Steel has always endeavored the best HR practices that start right from an ideal system of recruitment. Recruiting right people for right job avoids most of the later conflicts and disputes at workplace and help boost employees' intrinsic motivation and morale.[50]

When it comes to initiatives regarding employee relations, employee development and growth, Tata Steel is of the opinion that people are its greatest asset and has therefore adopted the best practices for its employees in this context too. It encourages trade unions considering them as the great assets to the organization. They are therefore present at all Tata Steel locations. Tata Steel is also a pioneer of joint consultation in its home country India for about 56 years now. Under joint consultation management of the company and employee representatives consult each other at all levels to discuss and address important issues related to company's progress, prosperity, production, productivity, safety, welfare, quality etc.[51]

Company has fully fledged grievance handling mechanism under which all grievances and complaints of employees are handled through an easy and well defined mechanism. Furthermore, company continuously works toward improving workplace standards to ensure better employee welfare. A unique program on Wellness@Workplace has been launched including health check ups and preventive health surveillance measures to confirm good health of employees across the company. In order to help employees go further in their professional growth company provides monetary incentives to employees who acquire higher technical qualification in related fields. On an equal and non discriminatory basis Tata Steel offers continuous skill and competence upgrading of all employees and provide access to necessary learning opportunities to them.

Tata Steel has its well established in house training facilities. TMDC (Tata Steel Management Development Center) is responsible to provide all managerial and functional training to employees and managers at different levels.

Other initiatives that promote employee professional growth include 70:20:10 learning and development program. The program institutes the notion that employees should be trained, coached and mentored in the systematic manner which enables them to further grow in their career and make them competent to take up higher level responsibilities. Under this program learning and development (L&D) is supported seventy percent through real life and on the job experiences, tasks and problem solving. Twenty percent L&D takes place through coaching, mentoring, discussions and guidance by superiors and experts whereas ten percent of L&D comes from class room instructions and sessions. There is provision of effective system of job rotation and career planning of the employees to ensure development of officers that improve their chance of retention with the company for the longer period of time.[52]

With the view to capture employee concerns and identify the need for policy changes 'Employee Contact Programme' was introduced in the year 2009. EDGE (Ensuring Development & Growth of Employees), the performance management system aligns the behavior and activities of all employees helping leaders to develop an ideal work culture, enhancing the performance and productivity and improving superior and subordinate relationships. Exclusively for women employees, Tata has launched number of initiatives like SWATI, the women empowerment cell that promotes development of women managers and employees with its various self development programmes.[53] List goes on of the initiatives that Tata Steel has adopted over the decades with respect to employee welfare, well being and satisfaction. This is the reason why Tata Steel employees show higher level of emotional attachment with the company by contributing their efforts and driving strong company performance with great revenues and profits.

Walmart

As the world's largest employer, Walmart employs more than two million employees across the world. Sam Walton, Wal-Mart's founder, valued his employees so great that he named Wal-Mart's HR department, The People Division, rather than the HR department. In order to achieve company's aggressive goals, Walmart employees work to their maximum capacity and efficiency to align organizational strategies and tactics together. Company's seven over riding strategies – price, operations, culture, key item/products, expenses, talent and service can only be implemented successfully by aligning HR practices with these strategic goals and targets of the company.[54]

Walmart has Benefits Team that works towards offering Walmart employees various comprehensive and affordable benefits that help them stay in good mental and physical health. Not only employees but their families can also be benefitted by number of initiatives Walmart has to offer with respect to their well being. Company has to offer different plans including Health Reimbursement Accounts plans and high deductible plan with Health Savings Account highlights of which include: 100 percent coverage for eligible in-network preventive care; $4 co-pay on eligible generic drugs at Walmart or Sam's Club pharmacies; Free access to nurse care managers and health care advisors; HMO plans (available in certain areas); Resources For Living® – a free confidential counseling and health information service; Company-paid life insurance; Accidental death & dismemberment insurance (AD&D); Critical illness insurance; Short- and long-term disability insurance; Business Travel Accident Insurance; Illness Protection (Sick Time) and Associate Eyewear Program. Apart from well being and health benefits, Walmart employees also enjoy financial benefits like: Matching contributions to employee's 401(k) up to 6% of the salary; Associate Stock Purchase Plan with a company match; Associate Discount Card for Walmart and Home Office associates and Sam's Club Home Office associates, spouses and dependents; Sam's Club associates receive a complimentary membership; Exclusive discounts on everything from brand new cars and wireless services to travel when associates visit Walmart's online Associate Discount Center – more than 375 discounts available.[55]

Walmart believes in continuous provision of training and development activities. Throughout employee's career he undergoes important competence and skill based trainings that help them to reach their fullest potential. For career growth and advancement Walmart offers various mentoring programs, sponsorships, leadership courses and associate resource groups etc. In order to develop managerial potential, company offers number of opportunities to sharpen leadership abilities and skills. For all salaried Walmart Stores U.S field associates, Assistant Management Training programs are conducted on great scale. To master the art of developing a unique culture in the company, Walton institute helps Walmart leaders through its specific education programs. Manager in training program at Sam's Club gives trainees the great exposure to different operations across various functional areas of the company. Walmart also partners American Public University which allows Walmart employees to receive college credit for their formal training and job experience at Walmart and Sam's Club.[56] Such sort of opportunities and benefits increase employees' sense of belonging with the company. When company offers so many benefits, make employee's life easy and also ensures their career growth, employees develop great emotional attachment with their organization. Over the years Walmart has very well retained its best talent by providing great emotional satisfaction to all its employees. It is evident by its position of largest employer with 2.2 million employees across the nations who are constantly contributing to Walmart's success as one of the topmost Fortune 500 global companies.

British Petroleum

British Petroleum being one of the most successful energy companies in the world offers the broad range of career aspirations. It has operations in 70 countries and nature of their business is extraordinarily complex that require constant and continuous innovation. BP employees get opportunity to work on world's most technically and commercially challenged projects in energy sector that enhance their self esteem and develop them to face and cope risks and challenges at various levels of business operations.[57]

BP fosters culture of collaboration and respect by encouraging team work, cross functional, cross countries and even cross continents operations. They reward the collective success that motivates employees to work more efficiently in teams. This also helps employees develop good relationships with team members and other concerned people satisfying their relatedness needs giving them more emotional satisfaction from their work. Individually, they are respected and recognized for their skills and expertise. Their opinion matters for BP. They are treated with genuine consideration are encouraged to share their thoughts. BP offers number of career friendly policies that also provide flexibility to work on career progress without compromising with family and professional life balance.[58]

In more than 70 countries BP employs nearly 86000 people. They operate in different cultures and environments and hence they encourage diversity that reflects BP's strength to have access to different societies across the globe. Their prior concern remains building employee's capability and rewarding them in most satisfying manner. Engaging with its people is equally important for BP. They conduct the annual survey to assess and monitor employee's level of engagement to identify areas where they need to improve. Employees are importantly measured on BP's strategic priority areas – safety, trust and value as to how engaged employees are with respect to these concerns. Also, employee's level of emotional satisfaction is measured through employee and workplace satisfaction indicator.[59] BP's concern for employee's engagement and workplace satisfaction give employees great feeling of being valued and enhance their level of belongingness with the organization.

In order to stay globally competitive BP encourage diversity and inclusion by creating a network of diversity and inclusion champions across the world who help BP manage diversity and create synergies out of inclusion of diverse workforce at various locations. To promote women employees BP has set a goal of gender representation in leadership position. According to this they plan to have 25% of group leaders and 30% of senior level leaders to be women by the year 2020.[60]

BP has a well defined system of rewarding performance. Performance is not only rewarded individually but there is provision to reward performance at three levels. One, the performance of the BP group overall, two the performance of the immediate part of the company where employee works and three at specific individual level. This type of system encourages employee to demonstrate his excellence to work as an individual player, the team member and BP employee who are employed to contribute to overall success of the organization. They are not only rewarded on what they deliver but also on how well they reflected BP values pertaining to safety, compliance and risk management.[61]

BP builds capabilities through number of initiatives at different levels due to its need of highly skilled people in specialized areas. They have system of structured recruitment that allows them to recruit right talent in right area of requirement focusing also on building talent from within the organization. When it comes to talent management, BP has world class opportunities for its employees. It has partnered with nineteen institutes and academies that deliver high quality technical learning and development. Every employee at BP is required to take at least five days training a year. BP also opens the opportunities to those engaged in complex functions to move into management and leadership positions. To prepare them for the same BP give them support through leadership development programs tailored as per specific management and leadership skill requirements of BP.[62]

Company also has great exported expertise as the BP expatriate employees are encouraged to distribute critical skills across locations and promote nurturing talent around the world through international assignments. Employee safety is paramount to BP values and operations and to ensure that BP organizes to put right people with right capabilities and experience in safety critical roles. In order to reinforce BP values in appropriate manner and achieve consistently safe, compliant and reliable operations, BP has specific programs to offer. In their safety and operation risk function they are focusing to hire more and more experienced and specialized candidates from external sources. BP is thriving to strengthen its capabilities and consolidation of their competence management program.[63]

BP's great emotional concerns in the areas of rewarding performance, managing talent, developing leaders, ensuring safety etc. help employees to feel more valued. They feel more cared and such positive emotion stimulators motivate them to contribute their full potential to achieve BP goals in most efficient manner.

Samsung Electronics

Process of managing human resources starts from planning of HR needs and then recruitment. Samsung follows an efficient recruitment process using various sources like internship programs, overseas recruiting, career forums etc. They generate huge pool of specialized candidates through these sources and then make most appropriate selections suitable for various needs of the organization. These selected employees then are put to most ideal and pleasant work environment that enhances their level of emotional satisfaction making their performance more effective.

There are special provisions for female workers to prevent them from career interruptions due to child care obligations. Samsung has introduced a trial run of a work at home/telecommuting system. A standardized process is developed to support people joining back from extended child care leave especially women under which career coaching is made available tailored for various career and needs of women employees. In order to promote gender based diversity Samsung is focusing on increasing the proportion of women employees in coming years. Company promotes diversity both in terms of product development and management of human resources. They have absolutely non discriminatory hiring policies that encourage foreign nationals, women, disabled and minority groups to apply and get better jobs with Samsung. In order to promote the global diversity Samsung has designed the reverse deployment scheme under which personnel from overseas subsidiaries are dispatched directly to Korea. This initiative was introduced to promote international knowledge and information exchange resulting in more creative and sustainable strategy formulation. A separate help desk is being operated to assist these personnel to adjust their works in the international environment and to offer other related programs. Samsung also provides special facilities to disabled employees and other minority groups. They are increasing their hiring of disabled workers and modifying relevant regulations and improving their existing facilities to make work experience better of disabled employees.[64]

In order to enhance quality of work life and maintaining work and life balance Samsung has introduced a flexible time program for administrative staff wherein they can set and manage their own work hours. Working hours in international subsidiaries are set and managed according to the local employment standards and guidelines. Samsung believes in providing such an ideal work environment to employees that they hardly feel the need of labor union at all. Still company has labor council in all their sites across the globe to facilitate necessary dialogue between labor and management. Underlying philosophy of the company with respect to human resources states that to attain mutual advancement, workers and company both will cooperate to adhere to company's principles of co-existence, co-prosperity and harmony. Samsung through its retirement and outplacement program provide assistance to retiring employees find new jobs or start their own business. This support is made available through career development centers.[65]

Samsung provides its employees all benefits required by law and also the internal benefits that help employees make their quality of life better. These benefits are available for all who are regular and even those who work on contract with the company. Some of the benefits are: group insurance, financial aid for medical costs, congratulatory/condolence pay and use of leisure facilities. In 2010 Samsung implemented the system of accumulated annual salary for individual workers that help in differentiating the compensation according to the performance of the employee. There is proper and well maintained system of grievance redressal where employees can report their grievances or submit suggestions through intranet and well maintained portals. Employee's grievances are promptly responded by general affairs, HR and other related departments on regular basis.[66]

Samsung offers wide range of training and development opportunities to its employees. According to the job functions, individual capabilities are assessed and to fulfill the requirement then training programs are designed to help employees gain expertise in related areas. In order to help employees based overseas company has provision of global education portal and mobile education system. Samsung makes every possible effort to ensure safe and pleasant work environment with number of health benefits available to Samsung employees. All of their production plants have obtained OHSAS18001 certification for occupational health and safety management system and also commission the leading international environment consultancy. Company through its health research center continuously works on employee health and well being research projects. To cope with emotional and psychological problems like strain and stress company is planning to expand its system of evaluation to check such problems and help employees enjoy their work and personal lives. There is also provision of professional counseling for those who need it to nurture a healthy and productive life. Furthermore there are special customized programs like smoking cessation, weight loss and emotional health to promote better and pleasant work environment by ensuring good employee health. To check the spinal health, there is fully fledged facility, center for prevention of musculoskeletal diseases which engages in diagnosing related problems and provides curative support.[67] Samsung takes care of employee's financial needs, emotional needs, time, health, career and their families and also ensure great work and life balance.

Toyota Motors

In order to help employees work on their full potential with great confidence, vigor and enthusiasm, Toyota believes in creating highly positive work environment. Company fosters great sense of pride and loyalty and encourages the culture of teamwork with healthy competition and effective communication.

An internal campaign called WE LOVE TOYOTA has been carried out since year 2009 with the vision to develop employee's interest in company's operations and to deepen their loyalty toward Toyota as their employer. Toyota also strives to promote the team and sport spirit. Company has 35 clubs consisting advanced athletes who compete for national championships. All employees get highly encouraged and motivated seeing these champions performing really well on behalf of the company. Toyota's women's softball club and men's basketball club Alvark won national championship in November 2011 and April 2012, respectively. Toyota understands the value of customer satisfaction for the business success and believes that customer satisfaction can never be ensured without employee satisfaction. To understand whether Toyota employees are emotional satisfied with the company or not, they conduct regular employee satisfaction surveys. Analysed results of the survey are used in planning and executing measures to help employees to have better quality of work life and great confidence in their organization.[68]

To establish efficient system of communication and good interpersonal relationships company has adopted range of initiatives. One such initiative is the lunchtime discussions with foreign staff regarding issues and differences they experience with respect to culture, personal trouble and worries, way of thinking of others etc. This practice nurtures great sense of being valued and deepens mutual trust and understanding between local and foreign employees. As a matter of fact, with respect to relationship with employees, Toyota's action principles 'Continuous Improvement' and 'Respect for People' have always served as two important pillars. Respect for people also refers to respect for all stakeholders and concern for employees is always of paramount importance for the company.[69] This assumptions is the actual genesis of my study and purpose of this book which emphasize that 'people' in business are not only employees or customers, but are all stakeholders that contribute together to business success and they need to be managed efficiently by high levels of emotional intelligence as big Fortune 500 companies do.

360 Degrees Implementation of Emotional Intelligence in Business

One of my studies '360 Degree EI Implementation Business Model – Tool to Achieve Competitive Advantage for Small, Medium and New Enterprises', which is published in the International Journal of Management (IJM)[70] tries to set instance before new, small and medium entrepreneurs to help them to achieve fast and sustainable growth with the use of EI. In order to reach to the purpose we investigated the EI based strategies successful corporations implement to achieve competitive advantage. This study has been divided in two parts. One, the comparative analysis of five global fortune 500 companies on the basis of how they are using EI to as a tool to achieve competitive advantage in business and second, develop the EI specific business model for new, small and medium enterprises.

Comparative study of corporations show how similar companies are in using EI practices to manage relationships with all their stakeholders. Study also revealed that these companies use EI strategies in different combination and compositions. Some companies are more concerned about their consumers and use more EI based practices to attract customers whereas some companies put more emphasis on the emotional satisfaction of their employees. Hence companies are, in some way similar and in other way different in how they use EI as a tool to achieve competitive advantage. Scientific methods were used to make the comparisons which empirically proved the findings of the study. The investigation clears that companies intensively use emotional intelligence based practices and this is the unique feature all successful companies have in common. And hence a suggestive '360 Degree EI Implementation Business Model' was developed for new, small and medium enterprises to achieve fast sustainable growth. Model suggests that just like big successful fortune 500 companies, new, small and medium scale entrepreneurs should also use EI as the tool to achieve competitive advantage. This model is expected to help these entrepreneurs and leaders ensure smooth business functioning with high level cooperation from the side of all business stakeholders. No stakeholder takes the risk to make contribution to specific business until he confirms his interests and motives are in right sync with business purpose and that business also has reward that he expects in return. Similarly stakeholders who are not directly associated with business (communities, government, and society at large) also accept business as the part of their system only when it confirms certain required ethical and concerned behavior. As a matter of fact this association of motives and social acceptance is based upon how effectively companies can satisfy emotions of the concerned parties that are stakeholders.

When we talk about satisfaction of emotions of the human resources of the company, various initiatives can be adopted to make employees feel positive emotions like happiness, joy, ecstasy, gaiety, bliss, elation, delight etc. Similarly when consumer buys a product he wants to fulfill his emotional needs along with fulfilling basic utility needs associated with the products. Along with focus on utility therefore, companies also try hard to ensure to satisfy some important consumer emotions like – fondness, attraction, adoration, sentimentality, caring etc. Moreover other stakeholders like governments, communities and society need companies to behave in most responsible way so as to avoid all sort of negative externalities caused by businesses. These parties also have their motives associated directly or indirectly with the business which when fulfilled or unfulfilled result in positive or negative generation of emotions. Investors, shareholders when investing in business expect to earn money or share company's profit and as they play very significant role in business growth they should also be confirmed proper returns on their investments. Third parties like suppliers, vendors, contractors etc. also have their motives associated with the business and every party finally needs positive fulfillment of the motives they have with the business.

Emotions are basically the outcomes of the motives. Motives or our expectations decide the emotions we feel and experience. If motives are fulfilled in a positive manner they will result in positive emotions which confirm the positive behavior too. For example if motives of employees are fulfilled, their productivity will enhance, if it happens with consumers their brand loyalty will get strong, investors and shareholders will make more investments more frequently and third parties also perform the way they are expected to if they find their motives aligned with company they are working with. This is how businesses achieve great success by providing emotional satisfaction to stakeholders through satisfying their motives. All stakeholders when perform with full motivation businesses grow more quickly and this is the lesson which new, small and medium scale entrepreneurs should learn.

Small and medium enterprises in India contribute to 22% of GDP. Despite this great contribution it is felt that small and medium enterprises in India face number of problems including strong competition with multinational corporations. Apart from the benefits of economies of scale, MNCs as discussed in our comparative analysis use great level of emotional intelligence to ensure sustainable business growth. Taking that comparative analysis as the pilot study, 360 Degree Emotional Intelligence Model of Business Development has been developed to guide new, small and medium level entrepreneurs to the path of sustainable business growth and development.

The model is based on the assumption that all stakeholders in the business have almost equal contribution in business growth and development. Considering it as the 360 degree coverage, the area of 60 degrees has been allotted to each segment of stakeholders. It is shown as 360 degrees EI umbrella coverage. Although umbrella shape covers only 180 degrees and suppose to protect us from rains showering from the sky (somewhere top), what if you also have water splashing from the bottom? You need then to have 360 degrees protection. If we create an EI umbrella which is made up of two umbrellas joint in a way that it becomes a complete spherical shaped envelope, businesses can protect themselves from negative environmental forces, hitting business from all the directions. Even if business is functioning in highly adverse conditions, it can be protected if its stakeholders provide constant support and this can happen only when they are emotionally attached with the business. EI based strategies should be implemented to manage emotions of all stakeholders as contribution of every single stakeholder is equally important and this is what big Fortune 500 companies are doing.

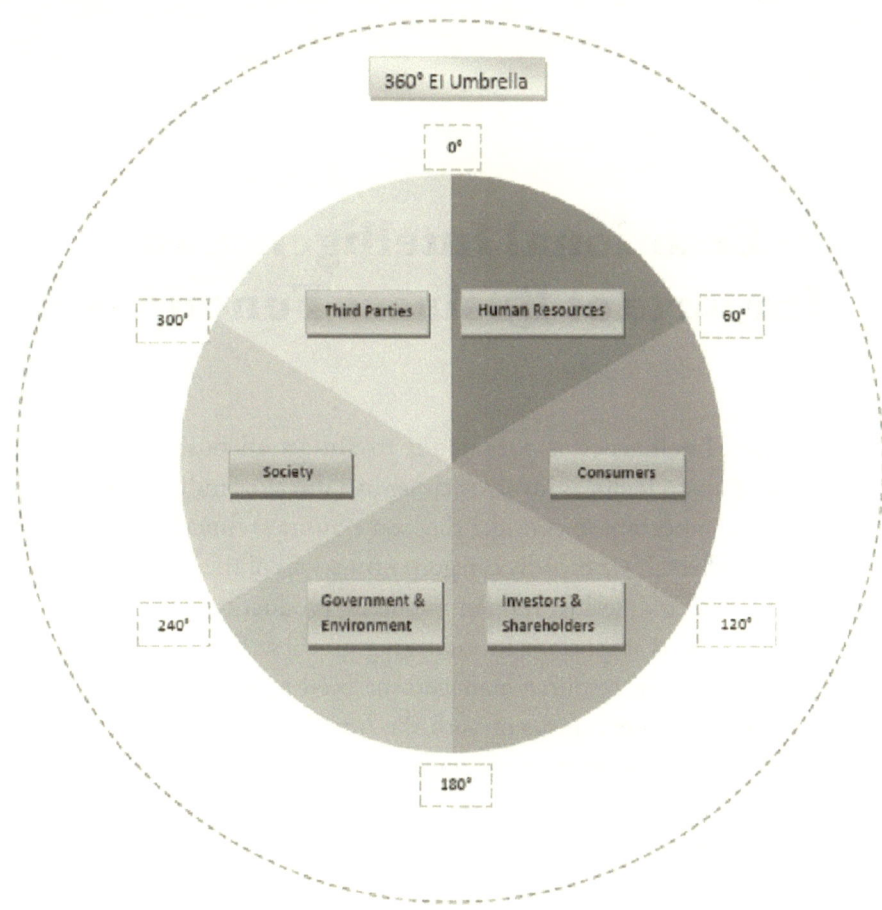

Figure 3 - 360 Degree EI Implementation Business Model

Emotional Intelligence in Important Business Functions

Emotional Intelligence is paramount to almost all business functions wherever the human factor is involved either in a direct or indirect manner. It is however also important to consider that some business functions need more EI focus than others. If we broadly categorize functions of the business they are managing finance, marketing, human resources, productions and operations. Although EI focus is important in managing all these functions effectively, marketing and human resource management need to have special EI focus as one of the fundamental tasks of both the functions is to manage 'human behavior' to achieve business goals and objectives efficiently. In following sections we are going to discuss some emotional intelligence perspectives to manage marketing and human resources (with special focus on behavioral dynamics and leadership) for business.

Marketing and Emotional Intelligence

No business can achieve success without proper marketing of its offerings. Marketing helps businesses to reach to the final consumers of the products and services and helps also in retaining existing customers with business. The main purpose of marketing is to generate more sales by product, price, promotion and place specific strategies. It keeps focused on building brand image and developing brand equity. At the nucleus of the marketing there lies the customer and hence at every step of marketing process, managers have to be aware of tactics that capture emotional attention of the customers. Marketing strategies of business are composed of number of emotional intelligence initiatives that help business to attract customer emotions resulting in sales at larger scales.

Emotional intelligence approach of marketing is divided into two parts:

➢ EI Thinking
➢ EI Action

To probe better into the concept 'EI Model of Marketing' is developed by integrating Victor Vroom's expectancy theory of motivation and EI principles. Victor Vroom has suggested that beliefs about expectancy, instrumentality and valence create a motivational force by a psychological interaction amongst these elements. Expectancy can be considered as different expectations and confidence levels about what an individual is capable of doing. Instrumentality refers to the perception of person that he will receive the reward if performance expectation is met. In other words it is his concern that for his performance or action, whether he will receive what he desires or not? Valence is the emotional orientation of the person he holds with respect to the outcomes or rewards. Eg. the depth of the want of a worker for remuneration.

As a matter of fact, three motivation elements – expectancy, instrumentality and valence have direct relationship with emotional states of human mind. As human emotions change situation to situations his level of expectancy, instrumentality and valence also change accordingly. Motivation itself is an important emotion state and is associated directly to the motives that person needs to achieve at a particular time. When these motives get fulfilled, he feels motivated by drive generated by his emotions.

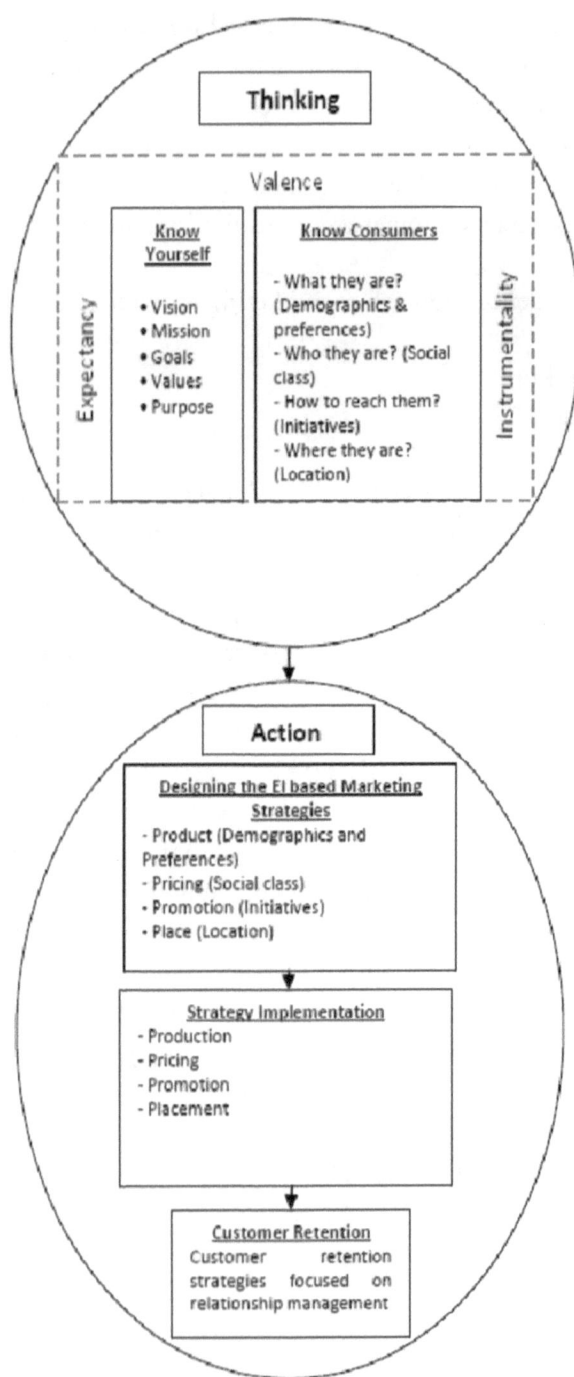

Figure 4 EI Model of Marketing

EI model of marketing is divided into two sections depicted in two circle shaped envelopes. First circle constitutes of 'thinking' whereas second one includes the action part. Thinking circle manifest the concept that thinking done in emotional intelligent way should be the first and foremost stage of marketing process which includes thinking about self and about consumers who are the final target of business. Main purpose of all marketing activities is to earn more revenues and profit by implementing appropriate marketing strategies.

Integration of Vroom's motivation elements signifies that business's vision, mission, goals, values and purpose all should generate proper expectancy, instrumentality and valence for consumers that can motivate them to buy their products over the competitors. Expectancy in this context refers to different expectations and levels of consumer's confidence resulted by his buying power of what he is capable of buying. Instrumentality on the other hand is the belief that a consumer will receive a reward in form of fulfillment of his want from the product provided by utility of the products and finally valence refers to the emotional orientations consumer holds with respect to outcomes or rewards e.g. the depth of the want of specific product.

So, motivation factor is an outcome of expectancy multiplied by instrumentality and valence. Absence of any of the element would result the zero motivation force. Strategy of marketing originally starts from initial stages of business planning. Therefore, while developing business's vision, mission, goals, values and purpose it is necessary to consider that all three elements of motivation (expectancy, instrumentality and valence) should be present in order to motivate consumers to buy our products.

While thinking about self, focus should be set on acquiring all the relevant knowledge about company's/business's vision, mission, goals, values and purpose and to ensure that all that are aligned with characteristics of customers business is targeting. A broken lined envelope covering 'know yourself' and 'know your consumers' rectangles shows that thinking about self and consumers should provide proper knowledge that whether business's self can motivate business consumers by appropriate levels and amounts of expectancy, valence and instrumentality elements of motivation or not.

Along with knowing the self, it is equally important to know about your consumers – what they are? This question answers the demographic characteristics and preferences of the consumers on the basis of which business can decide what products are to be produced. Who they are? Question clears what social class do targeted customers belong to and this helps to determine prices of the product. How to reach them? Different ways, routes, means and measures are there to reach to a specific group of consumers, and it is important for business to know what exactly the right method to reach consumers is. Where they are? Various locations, regions, geographical areas need to be identified where targeted consumers can be found to facilitate proper distribution of the product.

After emotion focused thinking, it comes to the action part which also needs to have a mindful approach of attracting consumers and ensuring good customer lifetime value.

Market research with focus on specific 'Ps' of marketing is the first step in action process with the help of which marketing strategy should be designed in an emotional intelligent manner. In order to understand what features product should have and what utility it should provide to consumers, research is done on consumers' demographics and preferences. Product type is decided on the basis of utility product is expected to deliver to the consumers. So how would business come to know what utility their product should be able to deliver? This is where market research comes into place. Market research starts usually with consumer research focused on consumer demographics and preferences. Consumer demographic information includes characteristics and features of the targeted population that helps business know what significant features should be there in the product that are suitable for the population with specific characteristics. Age, income, gender, height, ethnicity, family structure, country, region are some of the demographic elements which can determine the product features. As a matter of fact, product features should be in perfect sync with the population features for eg. If average height of population is five feet and five inches, a dress manufacturing business should manufacture dresses in size that is suitable for the people of this average height. Similarly, in order to decide upon specific product features, consumers' preferences are researched which are subject of number of factors like choices, tastes, beliefs, values, attitudes, cultures etc.

With respect to 'product', consumer preferences determine what type of product business should produce. Consumers buy products that bring them happiness and contentment or at least either of one. Preferences however are first determined by product's utility for a consumer and then other factors fall in place like consumer choice, taste, beliefs, attitudes, values, culture, religion etc. For example, in summer season person is feeling thirsty and has two choices to quench his thirst - water and energy drink. To reach to his office, he needs to walk further a mile. He therefore decides to opt energy drink as along with satisfying the thirst, it will also provide him energy to put some more physical effort. Here his preference was subject to the utility of the product that is the drink that quenches the thirst and provides energy. When he went to the shop he saw number of energy drinks kept in the shelf and he picked orange flavored drink with a good brand. Now, his choice was influenced by his taste and preference to specific brand (know more in 'The emotional intelligent branding'). Brand preference as a matter of fact, is associated to the fulfillment of individual's higher order needs that have direct relation with emotional fulfillment of specific desires.

In marketing mix, product pricing is another significant factor which is having emotional relevance for consumers. Pricing strategies adopted by business could be any one or combination of following strategies:

- Market penetration
- Skimming
- Competitive
- Product line
- Bundle
- Psychological

Market penetration pricing strategy is an emotional tool attracting customers by low prices of the products. Product prices are kept lower than competitors to attract consumers to opt same product in lesser price. Every consumer needs to achieve maximum satisfaction from each unit of money he spends to buy a specific product. If he finds product that fulfils his utility, consists of all features he wants to be there in the product, and the product is available in comparatively low prices, consumer gets emotionally inclined to purchase that product. This type of pricing strategy basically focuses on generating awareness of the product in the market but needs to be carefully implemented as sometimes businesses failed to earn required revenue and profits if they set prices too low.

Skimming on the other hand is the pricing strategy whereby businesses focus to price their product at highest initial price with the view that when demand of one set of customers gets fulfilled, next set of customers will be charged comparatively lower price. Skimming word signifies business's strategy to skim the top layer of cream that is customers on top level of social class. This type of strategy has its own drawbacks and can be implemented only if you have sufficient number of customers in top market segment who prefer to buy your product over your competitors. At the same time this pricing strategy helps generate good emotional value in a way that many times customers perceive highly priced commodities as high quality resulting high customer preference for that product.

Competitive pricing is the strategy wherein prices of the product are set almost similar to that to the competitor. This strategy is usually implemented to the product having number of substitutes with similar product features offered to the same market segment. In this case business does not have any choice but to charge what competitor is charging. Customers find no big difference in prices and opt for the product on the basis of small product differentiation. Product line pricing is adopted in a case when business decides to offer products on different price points in the same product range. This type of pricing is adopted when product comes with new and upgraded features on the basis of which higher price could be charged. Latest mobile phone pricing is the good example of this type of pricing strategy. Mobile phones initial models are charged lesser but as they get more customized and new features are added to the sets, their prices go higher. In such sort of cases consumer preference depends on – first, brand is already an established brand which has proven its quality in the previous versions of the product and second, consumers do not mind to pay more for added features which attract them the most.

Bundle pricing is one of the most emotion oriented pricing strategies. In this type of pricing a bunch, packet or set of goods or services is offered at the price lower than the total price of all products if they are offered separately. Combo meals in fast food outlets and cinema halls are the good example of bundle pricing. Most of the consumers have limited purchasing power and product preferences but when a consumer finds in a bundle he is getting some products much less priced than offered separately, emotional demand generates and he decides to buy a bundle for the price which always has some good profit margin for the sellers and companies.

Psychological pricing is the other strategy that targets the consumer's emotions and based upon psychology of association. Consumer's psychology says 'less price better deal', as he associates less price with saving money and getting a better deal. When he finds product priced at $9.9 he associates it closer to $ 9 than $ 10. If product had offered for $ 10 its demand would suppose to be lesser than when it is priced at $9.9. Most of the companies nowadays are following this strategy as it works really great in attracting consumers by influencing their emotions over products that are so called less or reasonably priced.

Pricing strategy may it be of any type, is adopted by businesses to influence emotions of targeted market segment and to attract more and more consumers willing to buy their products. Price as a matter of fact is one of the most important factors that affect consumer's preference for specific product. Price is money, money is earned by spending time and effort and consumer perceives his earned money as reward of his work. When it comes to spend this earned reward, customer usually gives thought as to what would be the best purchase that fulfils his demand and costs the minimum. Businesses therefore price their offerings with due attention to provide emotional satisfaction to the consumers.

Place or product distribution is the next component of marketing mix strategy. Placement deals with distributing product to the places where they can easily get accessed by consumers. Emotional intelligence principles relevant to consumers say that as per consumer's psychology, they prefer to buy products that are easily accessible by them and are under their reach of physical locations (until and unless it is matter of some unique choice). Consumers never want to get to faraway places to make their purchases as it takes more time, money and effort. This is the reason why there are large number of online stores opened today. Almost all types of products consumers can buy online as it saves their time, money and effort and leave them more emotionally satisfied. This online retailing and trading saga has changed entire picture of business today. The moment you log on some website, attractive advertisements, offers capture your attention. You want or not, you finally end up buying the product as you also consider you need not to move somewhere to collect what you have bought and product you can get right at your doorstep.

Promotion is one 'P' of marketing mix that needs most of emotional intelligence focus to succeed. It is an effective combination of promotional methods used to attract customer's attention toward the specific product. Attention can be captured only by stimulating emotions and feelings and hence due importance is given to devise promotional strategies that ensure maximum customer attention lead to volume sales. Promotion mix includes:

- Personal selling
- Advertising
- Direct marketing
- Sales promotion
- Public relation

Personal selling includes one-to-one communication between seller and prospective buyer. It helps to generate direct contact with prospective and existing customers and hence is considered as one of the most effective tools of promotion strategy. Personal selling involves personal contact and customer feels more valued when contacted on an individual basis. This involves personal meetings, telemarketing, e-mails, and correspondence which sometimes cost companies more due to one to one approach of contacting the prospects. Also it takes more time and effort as compared to other promotional techniques. Despite all drawbacks, personal selling is used intensively by corporations as it generates the strongest emotional value for the customers by making them feel valued and important.

Unlike promotion, advertising is a form of non personal promotion. It is when companies pay to promote ideas, goods, or services with the use of a variety of media types. Advertising basically deals with making potential customers aware of the offerings of the business but is not as easy to produce as it seems to be. Corporations hire advertising agencies to make advertisements for them. These agencies have best of creative people to work on ideas that attract potential customers toward the specific product. Advertising is a message from producer to consumer about how his products are going to benefit the consumer if they buy them. In order to communicate this message a very well planned and designed advertisement is required to be produced. Following are certain decisions that affect advertisement production:

- Who are the potential consumers (market segment)
- Advertisement budget
- Purpose of advertisement (usually profits)
- Message to be communicated (the message strategy)
- Choice and cost of media
- Selection of media

In production of an advertisement other than the advertisement budget and media decisions, all decisions need to be taken and viewed in an emotional intelligent manner. First of all it is important to know who exactly your target consumers are. Not only their demographic information you need to have, you also should know what their preferences, choices, interests are. This we have already discussed in previous sections how consumer preferences, choices, values, purchasing power, and culture affect their buying decisions.

Purpose of advertisement should be very clear while planning an advertisement. One such purpose could be enhancing goodwill of the business as strong goodwill is always needed for sustainable development and growth of the business. Also, certain corporations advertise for social cause too which needs advertisement to be made absolutely with the different outlook. It is therefore very important to have a well defined purpose of the advertisement you are planning to produce. Launching absolutely new product or introducing new to the existing product line? Advertising business to business or business to consumers? Advertising locally, regionally, nationally or internationally? These could be some other questions related to purpose specific advertisement strategy. On the basis of purpose then it is decided that what message is needed to be communicated through advertisement. For example if purpose of advertisement is to sell business to business, message in advertisement will be designed to attract emotions of business entrepreneurs rather than common public. Similarly if it's the case of business to consumer product, message will be designed to attract emotions of common public and consumers in general.

Business to consumer advertisement is different from business to business advertisement where direct message is sent to prospective buyer through advertisement. In this situation, businesses focus on public in common. Message of advertisement also is selected focusing potential consumer's emotions in mind. Usually in magazines, hoardings and other displays you see pictures of beautiful women with an attractive features showing how some specific product has contributed to their beauty and poise. Also there are catchy taglines that capture human attention and emotions in most rapid manner. Such B2C ads are more general in nature rather than specific B2B advertisements.

Choice and cost of media and finally selecting the media are other concerns of advertisement strategy. Choice basically is made on the basis of approach of specific media to targeted market segment. Products that are targeted to masses in general are usually advertised on television and radio which are though expensive but are most effective means to reach to the common public. When consumer segment is specific for example the business students, business magazines, newspapers and websites can be selected considering almost all business students reads such sort of magazines and newspapers to keep abreast with latest information in business world.

Online advertisement is one such effective and successful ways of reaching to consumers anywhere in the world. Websites and corporations together devise most emotionally intelligent strategies to capture consumers sitting in their homes and workplaces. Popular websites like facebook and google are accessed by billions of users across the globe. Website asks user to mention his/her gender, age and other demographic information while creating the account on the website. Such information is then used by corporations and enables them to reach to their targeted market segment. A woman sitting in the United States, 35 years of age will come across most of the fashion products, accessories and apparel, mother and baby care products advertisements on her facebook page. These advertisements flashed everytime on the webpage emotionally force them to click the link leading them to the main website of the product loaded with all attractive offers alluring the customers to buy products online. Online advertisement has increased the rate of impulsive buying.

If you are a corporate employee and you constantly receive e-mails regarding offers of executive development programmes by universities and training institutes, you are being targeted under direct marketing strategy of these universities and institutions. Direct marketing is a type of advertising directed to a targeted group of prospects and customers rather than to a mass audience. Two forms of direct marketing are printed by mail, or direct by e-mail. The goals of direct marketing are to generate sales or leads. Direct marketing allows a business to engage in one-way communication with is customers about product announcements, special promotions, bulletins, customer inquiries, and order confirmations. This strategy generates emotional value in two ways. One when potential customer receives this sort of offer he takes pride to belong to special class of consumers. Second, the direct mail (printed or electronic) when received by consumers they feel to have more and individual attention rather than feeling of being approached in bulk.

Sales promotions are used to stimulate purchasing and sales and the objectives are to increase sales, inform potential customers about new products, and create a positive business or corporate image. Using coupons, schemes, free gifts, price offs, product samples, point-of-purchase displays to generate more sales are the examples of sales promotion initiatives. As a matter of fact sales promotion is highly emotion driven initiative of marketing. When consumer comes across such great offering like 30% off on weekend purchase of pizza, he thinks that he is saving great amount money on that specific deal. This emotional tendency motivates him to make purchase and he feels more emotionally fulfilled by that decision.

Public relations activities enable an organization to influence a target audience. Most of the time, public relation campaigns try to create a favorable image for a company, its products, or its policies. Something similar we have discussed in previous sections where we pointed companies' strategies and initiatives to create and sustain the positive image to emotionally attract consumers and other stakeholders to favor the business. Corporations get involved in number of CSR initiatives, sustainability measures, and environment friendly policies and use them as the tool of publicity. As a matter of fact publicity deals with bringing newsworthy information to the public. Through publicizing all such sorts of initiatives and achievements, companies attract stakeholders in different dimensions. Companies give news releases to announce newsworthy developments about a company's products or services, distribution channels, facilities, operations, partners, revenues and earnings, employees, and events. Publicity is one powerful tactic that public relations professionals use to stimulate feelings and emotions of targeted stakeholders (primarily customers) to ensure higher revenues, profits with sustainable growth and development of the business.

The Emotional Intelligent Branding

Brand is the significant feature of the product that is completely an emotional impression of the product in the mind of the consumer. Brand is product's identity that makes products distinct from each other. It is like an individual's identity comprises of different features, personality and association with certain community and society. Every business wants to establish as a successful brand in the market as consumers buy popular brands to fulfill both their lower order and higher order needs. What motivates consumer to buy a specific product is also the matter of hierarchy of his needs. In order to fulfill the physiological needs, consumer can just buy a product. But if he needs to buy a product that have high quality, he targets to fulfill safety needs by buying brand that ensures high quality. Also, if consumer belongs to a good social class, he would like to ensure that he buys the brand that matches his social class (social and relatedness needs). Now, if consumer has high purchasing power to buy a brand, he also tends to confirm that brand he buys should fulfill his esteem and self actualization needs too. Consumer as a matter of fact usually tries to satisfy as many levels of needs as possible with amount of money he has at disposal. He buys brands to satisfy his different lower order needs like physiological needs, safety, social needs and relatedness needs. At the same time the same purchasing power he also needs to fulfill his higher order needs that are esteem needs and self actualization needs. Most of the times, purchasing power of consumer decides what levels of different needs he can fulfill by his purchase.

If consumer has limited or less purchasing power, he would just be able to buy products may be very cheap brands by which he can just fulfill his physiological needs, but if he has some more money he can think of buying something with good quality and good brand that fulfills his safety and social needs. But if he has more disposable income he can think of buying expensive brands that satisfy his esteem and even self actualization needs. Other than physiological needs, all other needs are subject to emotions person has about fulfillment of needs. Safety, social, relatedness, esteem, self actualization are all felt in mind and outcomes of emotions person holds for something. If person decides to buy a brand that fulfils these needs, his emotions are responsible for all the decisions he takes in this regard.

Brand motivates consumers to buy the product by stimulating his emotions and this is the reason why corporations give due emphasis to branding and design branding strategies in most emotional intelligent manner.

Marketing function also puts significant emphasis on branding of the product. Branding deals with conversion of product into a specific brand and managed through brand management whereby managers implement number of strategies to make brands more successful in the market by using number of initiatives focused on emotions of consumers. Branding usually consists of following stages focused on consumer's emotions:

1. Product research
2. Product development

3. Product conversion to brand
4. Brand management strategy
5. Testing
6. Audit
7. Building connections
8. Brand promotion and awareness generation
9. Strategic brand customer relationship management
10. Strategic evaluation
11. Manage to sustain current position in the market

In the first stage of branding i.e. product research it is important to give due attention to the preferences of 'customer'. Research is done on the ideas to find the answer of the question same by every business - What to produce that attracts customer most? Number of techniques is used to know customer preferences. It could be a customer survey, observation, market research etc. that gives correct idea about what customers exactly want. Product and its features most preferred by the customers are usually chosen for the next stage of product development.

The stage of product development includes physical development of the product where 'customer' is kept in nucleus of each production phase. Customer make choices based upon certain considerations. First, Utility of the product is focused by customer and then he chooses to buy with good quality and reasonable price. Products are manufactured keeping utility, quality, preferences, choices, values, culture, and purchasing power etc. in view. After product is developed and take final shape brand managers move forward to convert the product into specific 'Brand'. They seek to add almost all attributes in brand that attract attention of potential buyer. The foremost task in this stage is to name the product. Name that is easy to understand, pronounce and memorize is selected. Brand name should easily be noticed by customers and its substance can be stored in human's memory that whenever required can be recalled instantly.

Product's design, weight, shape are some other concerns while making decisions pertaining to branding. Therefore, to ensure a good quality product, brand managers have to be very careful about all such concerns. Next comes the decision on logo of the brand. Logo usually is a graphic mark that represents the brand and gives specific recognition to the product. It is designed in such a way that it receives most of customer's focus. Attractive marks with appealing colors and structures are chosen to grasp customer's attention for the brand.

Establishment of brand essence is another task which needs much of customer centricity. Essence could be a statement or word connecting customer's emotions with brand. For example: Raymond in India is selling brand with essence - 'The Complete Man' which gives man feeling of being a complete man resulting enhanced brand preference of this product amongst men. Essence help customer to choose products most suitable for his emotional preferences and confirms long term relationship bond between customer and brand. Selection of words is of paramount value here. Words which strike customer's mind and capture their attention for brand are chosen after due scrutiny. Words can be in form of slogan, a punch line or a tag line of the product. Brand managers select combination of most appealing combination of words that convey brand message to the customers. 'Life is good', LG's slogan gives consumer feeling of contentment with the brand as it generates the impression that it is LG product that makes life – a good experience. All these attributes added to brand in conversion process need high focus on customer's emotions and when utilized appropriately in building brand, confirm high level of customer satisfaction and lifetime value.

Next branding stage is brand management strategy that is designed to ensure that brand is able to consistently attracts the attention of maximum of targeted customers confirming good level of their loyalty. This stage enunciates making brand distinctive establishing its own unique identity with different brand associations and architecture. This is the way how customers will perceive brand as any one of: co – brand, which addresses similar need segment, multiple brand that gives each product a unique identity, fighting brand that comes up as a struggling and a new brand, house of brands consisting number of offerings with different brand names, branded house consisting number of offerings under same brand name, endorsed brands, sub brands etc. All these strategies are devised in order to maintain great customer relationship with unique and emotional brand identity.

After finalizing the appropriate strategy for brand architecture and management, managers start making preparations to launch the brand in market. First step here is testing of brand on specific customer segment with sample from respective population. Experiences of brand are then studied with brand audit. Brand audit is done to measure brands efficiency in satisfying customer's preferences for product utility, its design, visual, images, channels of distribution and goodwill it could build over time. Usually customer's response for brand is analyzed by mind mapping techniques, questionnaires, critical incident analysis etc. In next focus is set on identifying what product attributes can help promote the brand in the market. In this stage connections are built between customer's requirements, his beliefs and brand attributes so that high level of customer satisfaction can be ensured. This stage basically help to understand attributes that brand associate with respective customer's physical and emotional requirements which develop the base for further marketing and advertising promotions.

In order to make consumers aware of brand, building customer loyalty and product competitiveness, brand promotions are done. At this stage, brand awareness is generated using number of emotional intelligent initiatives. At the time of brand promotion customer databases are used to approach existing and potential customers customer relationship management softwares help to track customers in various locations and regions physical and virtual. Specific softwares use technology that traces customer's presence on specific websites. Finding them available on these sites companies send them advertisements and offerings which users can see on their respective webpages. This is how brands get their emotional existence marked in customer's mind.

Strategic Brand and customer Relationship Management stage comes next where efforts are made on strengthening customer relationships with business using combination of emotional intelligent strategies. These strategies focus on creating new customers, retaining existing customers, building loyalty and trust relationships and finally ensuring long term profitability. Having customer centricity in its nucleus, main purpose of marketing strategy is to align all organizational resources like personnel, operating practices and procedures, internal and external systems, products and services etc. in such a way that it will ensure mutual profitable relationship between organization and customers. Marketing strategy strongly emphasize on retention of existing customers as it is always cost effective to retain existing customers than creating new ones. An effective marketing strategy formulated in an emotional intelligent manner addresses almost all issues of corporate branding. It doesn't only bolster the strong customer loyalty by constantly approaching and serving the needs of consumers but also ensures long customer life time value by adequate attention to continuous customer satisfaction monitoring.

An important phase of strategic evaluation finally comes where efficacy of implemented strategies is measured. It can be considered in terms of investment in strategy implementation to sales volumes, profits, customer response to brand, customer lifetime value or combination of any or all the options. Before implementation of any strategy some standard parameters are set for performance measurement on the basis of which effectiveness of strategy implementation is measured. Irrespective of any measure, marketing strategy is considered to be successfully implemented if it could generate more revenues for the business. Higher revenues show that strategy achieved success in attracting emotions of the consumers motivating them to buy specific brand.

EI and CRM

Companies make great efforts to retain their existing customers considering retention is the better and more cost effective than creating new customers. Advertisement is an expenditure that needs to be made every time you tend to cater to new set of customers and is a continuous practice that keeps customer abreast with product offerings and keep him reminding – product exists. Where advertisement is considered to be such an important measure, it is an expensive affair too. There are instances of corporations which have not only survived but have earned huge profits with very less expenditure in advertisement. Harley Davidson is one such example. But what is there that support organizations to make revenues even in absence of extensive advertisement? It is customer relationship management or CRM. It is defined as –

'Customer relationship management (CRM) is a model for managing a company's interactions with current and future customers. It involves using technology to organize, automate, and synchronize sales, marketing, customer service, and technical support'.[71]

~ Shaw Roberts

The above definition explains CRM as business strategy that is fundamentally focused on managing interactions with existing and potential customers using technological support. Most of the definitions of CRM present almost similar impression that CRM is very much about using technology to interact with customers. However to define it in a complete manner we can say that CRM is the business strategy that has customer emotional value in focus, implemented using technology to manage better relationship with existing and potential customers.

Relationships can broadly be categorized in following ways:

Relationships based upon societal needs: established to fulfill societal norms (husband – wife, superior – subordinate, mentor – mentee etc)

Relationships based upon emotional needs: Made under psychological interests of love, association or benefit. (Lovers, friends, acquaintances etc.)

Relationship of business with its customers is second type where customers buy products for their benefits and once they find product fulfilling their physiological and emotional needs, they develop a relationship with the brand. Same way customer is the source of income (benefit) for the business and considering this, businesses seek to establish and develop long and loyal relationship with its customers. As this bond establishes on interests of both the parties, it is type of the relationship based upon the emotional needs. It is therefore primarily important for CRM experts and managers to understand the significance of emotions of their customers and clients to serve them better. As a matter of fact, company's CRM strategy is designed on the basis of its offerings and nature and type or customers it targets. Tata Steel Ltd being corporation with more 'business clients' needs to have different and comparatively low emotion focus in CRM than Toyota Motors, Samsung Electronics, British Petroleum and Walmart which supply products directly to the consumers.

The primary purpose of CRM is to ensure long lifetime value of the customers by communicating them the benefits they can enjoy being the loyal customers and not switching to other brands.

EI based Leadership to Manage Productivity, Performance and Behavior

Leaders need to understand that in order to ensure effective organizational performance, they need to confirm high level employee productivity. As a matter of fact employee performance is measured in terms of his level of productivity. Emotional intelligence play pivotal role in managing individual productivity in his personal and professional life settings. Important productivity concerns for an employee include – the *efficiency* to attain organizational goals and the *effectiveness* in terms of quality, quantity, cost and time considerations of the organization. It is proved by studies that individual productivity levels go down when feels bad emotions and get into the state of depression. In case of extreme stimulus in a negative form, part of brain responsible for conscious control and decision making shuts down. Hormone called cortisol is produced by human body in such situation that results in increased blood pressure, increased blood sugar and suppressed immune system. Specific physiological consequences of emotional distress are: fatigue, chest pain, sleeping problems, stomach upset, change in sex drive, muscle tension/pain and headaches. Psychological consequences include difficulty in thinking in a logical and sequenced manner, difficulty in decision making, forgetfulness, difficulty in concentration, sadness or depression, irritability or anger, lack of motivation or focus, restlessness, anxiety etc. Emotional distress also has serious behavioral implications like overeating or undereating, angry outburst, drug or alcohol abuse, social withdrawal, poor work relations, sense of loneliness, decreased sex drive, failing to set aside time to relax etc. All these physiological, psychological and behavioral consequences of emotional distress affect employee productivity to the great extent. Employees can never perform on their maximum potential when they experience such adverse distress caused by negative emotions. It is therefore evident that emotions have strong impact over productivity and by controlling emotions, productivity of employees can be enhanced in an easy manner.

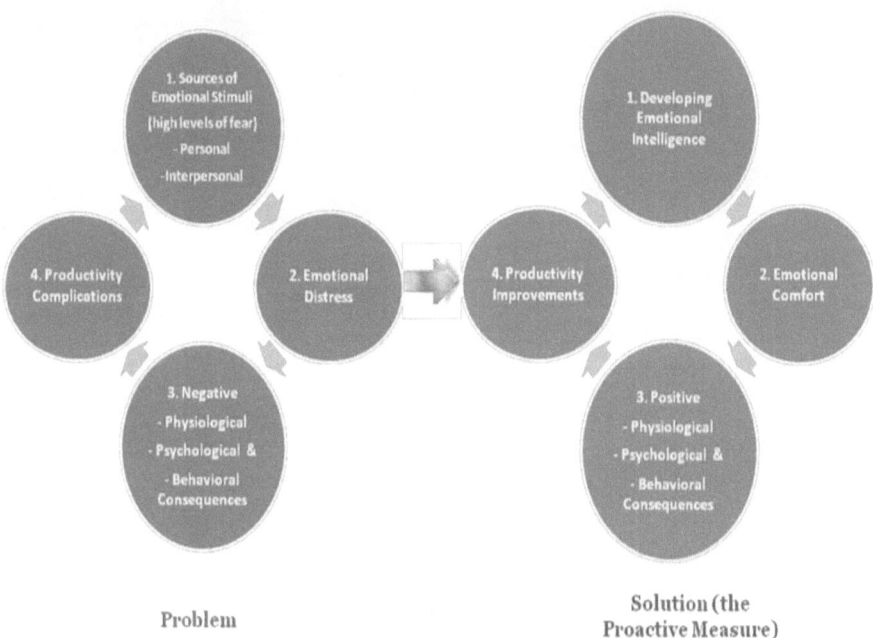

Problem

Solution (the Proactive Measure)

Figure 5 The Emotion Productivity Hookup

Figure 5 suggests how productivity can be enhanced by managing emotions of the employees. The model first shows the reasons or sources of emotional distress which may be the situation caused at intrapersonal level of individual (eg. conflict between his own core values, wants and needs) or it might be the problem individual faces due to his interpersonal dealings with other human beings. Such situations then cause emotional distress which can have number of physiological, psychological and behavioral consequences that finally lower down the levels of employee productivity as discussed above. In order to prevent such situation, leaders need to devise the proactive emotional intelligent strategies that help employees feel emotional comfort at workplace. Unlike emotional distress, emotional comfort helps employees experience the positive physiological, psychological and behavioral consequences that result high levels of employee productivity.

Now the question arises what are emotional intelligent strategies or how can they be designed to ensure efficient organizational productivity and performance? Emotional intelligent strategies focused on managing performance are EI based initiatives and actions that prevent the emotional distress and develop the culture of high emotional comfort at the workplace.

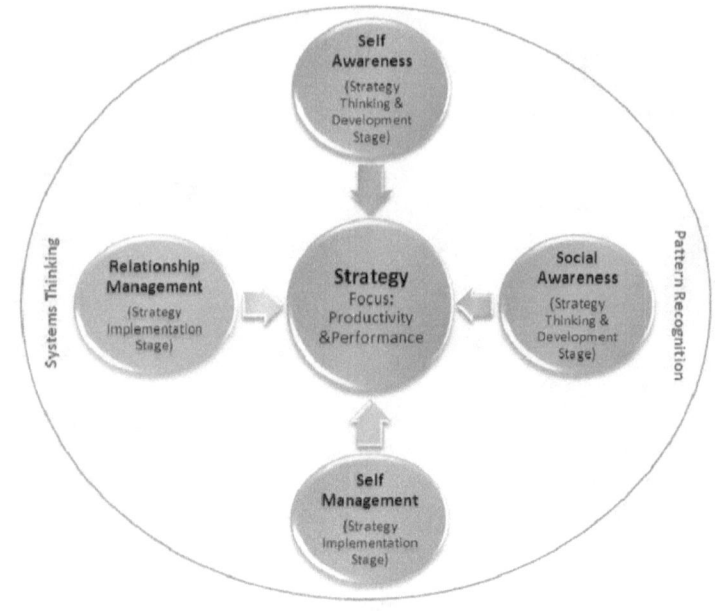

Figure 6 Strategic Framework of Productivity and Performance Management

In order to devise such sort of strategies, leaders need to develop certain specific competencies. Richard Boyatzis and Daniel Goleman developed the concept of specific emotional, social and cognitive intelligence competencies. Competencies as per their study are behavioral approach to emotional, social and cognitive intelligence. Emotional intelligence competencies are divided into self awareness and self management clusters. Self awareness cluster consists of emotional self awareness competency that deals with recognizing one's own emotions and their effects. Self management cluster on the other hand consists of four competencies. 1) Emotional Self Control which keeps the disruptive emotions and impulses in check. 2) Adaptability which enunciates person's ability to be flexible and handle change in different situations. 3) Achievement Orientation, person's tendency to strive to improve or meet the standards of excellence. 4) Positive Outlook that helps person see the positive aspects of things, situations and the future events. Social Intelligence competencies include social awareness and relationship management clusters. Social awareness cluster enunciates two competencies. 1) Empathy which is individual's ability to sense other's feelings and perspectives helping him to take active interest in their concerns. 2) Organizational Awareness that deals with reading group's emotional currents and power relationships. Relationship management cluster consists of five competencies. 1) Coaching and mentoring through sensing other's development needs and bolstering their performance and abilities. 2) Inspirational Leadership to guide individuals and groups. 3) Influence to wield effective tactics for persuasion. 4) Conflict Management to negotiate and resolve various disagreements. 5) Teamwork that deals with working together with people to achieve shared goals and creates synergies with combined efforts. Cognitive Intelligence competencies finally include: 1) Systems Thinking that deals with perceiving multiple causal relationships in understanding phenomena or events and 2) Pattern Recognition that perceives themes or patterns in seemingly random items, events or phenomena.[72]

In this study Boyatzis and Goleman have taken emotional and social competencies differently. However, social awareness and relationship management constructs are being included as specific emotional intelligence domains in different studies of Daniel Goleman. As per his competency framework there are four specific EI domains – Self Awareness, Social Awareness, Self Management and Relationship Management. These domains combinedly determine how effectively people can work with others and with the self.[73]

EI domains, competencies and cluster concepts propounded by Richard Boyatzis and Daniel Goleman are used here to develop the strategic framework that can be used by leaders to enhance levels of their employee's productivity and performance. Under this framework 'Strategy' focused on productivity and performance improvement is put in the core. It is shown that in order to develop an ideal productivity and performance boosting strategy leaders need to use their self awareness, social awareness, self management and relationship management competencies in combination of fundamental cognitive competencies. Strategic framework of productivity and performance improvement is shown in figure 6. In the framework - self awareness, social awareness, self management and relationship management are shown as surrounding core strategy components that need the primary focus in strategy building. Also while taking the strategic decisions leaders need to use proper system thinking and pattern recognition competencies. Self awareness as per this framework helps leaders to understand their personal and organizational strategic needs and requirements. Social awareness supports them with the understanding of others feelings, perceptions, needs, motives and behaviors that people can show in different situations.

It is important to note here that competencies in self awareness and social awareness domains are needed at the level of strategic thinking and development stage. At this stage very important strategic decisions are taken with respect to employee productivity and performance concerns which need proper knowledge of self and others in context. On the other hand self management and relationship management are considered to be useful at the strategy implementation stage where strategic decisions are put to practice. Leader's competencies of self management help him to practice emotional self control, adaptability, achievement orientation and positive outlook in a way that it helps him to remain efficient at every step of process of strategy implementation. Similarly, his relationship management competencies like coaching and mentoring, influence, inspirational leadership, conflict management and teamwork facilitate in creating culture of high level of trust and engagement boosting productivity and performance in most efficient manner.

Overall framework is covered with the cognitive competencies of systems thinking and pattern recognition that need to be involved in all stages of strategy thinking, development and implementation. System thinking helps in perceiving the reasons and consequences, causal relationships in various events and phenomena whereas pattern recognition competency supports in perceiving various themes and patterns around in random events and processes. These specific cognitive competencies need to be used equally at thinking, development and implementation stages of strategic framework due to their importance in rational decision making and behavior management concerns.

After discussing the strategic framework for productivity and performance management, let us now see a unique leadership model that helps in managing employee behavior at workplace.

It is always a challenging task to manage behavioral dynamics at workplace. Organization consists of integral human components who keep on interacting with each other in order to meet organizational and personal goals. In organizations people interact with two motives – one, to fulfill organizational goals and second to acquire personal satisfaction with informal bonds and relationships. Behavior of people in organizations completely depends upon motives of people as all behavior is result of motives. It is therefore very necessary for leaders to have sufficient knowledge of motives of his people so that he can easily manage their emotions. Emotional Intelligence plays pivotal role in managing interpersonal and intrapersonal relationships at workplace.

Human behavior in organizations has always remained area of great concern for strategy makers. Any strategy may it be related to production or distribution, marketing or finance need strong HR commitment and cooperation. 'Human' factor in organizations is the most vulnerable and challenging to manage resource due to their varied personalities and different motives. It has been proved by number of researches that most of the problems in organizations are result of conflicts caused by individual differences. Individuals are different on the basis of certain demographic factors, abilities and skills, perceptions, attitudes, personalities and their motives (purposes) in life.

When two persons come together to work for the common goal they exhibit individual differences sometimes in form of different personalities, perceptions, attitudes and sometimes their own specific motives. It is very important that motives of the organization and that of employees should be in sync in some or other way. But despite working for the same motive people face number of problems and they respond to same problems in very different way due to different personality traits. Personality traits that differentiate one person from other may be categorized as the extent to which person is:

- Open to experience,
- conscientious,
- extravert,
- agreeable,
- neurotic,
- possess self esteem,
- avoids harm,
- seeks novelty,
- seeks perfection,
- suffers alexithymia;
- psychoticism;
- obsession,
- rigid,
- impulsive, or

- shows disinhibition

All the above factors determine a person's response to specific stimulus. There has always been discussion on the fact that different people respond and behave to the same situation differently. This happens because they are different on the basis of above parameters. Also, different people communicate their behaviors in different manners.

Centre for Clinical Interventions, Australia elucidates three specific, usual behaviors people show via their communication patterns. These three behaviors are:[74]

1. Assertive;
2. Passive and
3. Aggressive

The Assertive Behavior

Person with this type of behavior communicates his feelings, thoughts, and beliefs in an open, honest manner without violating the rights of others

Verbal characteristics:

- Firm, relaxed voice
- Fluent, few hesitations
- Steady even pace
- Tone is middle range, rich and warm
- Sincere and clear
- Not over-loud or quiet
- Voice appropriately loud for the situation
- "I" statements ("I like", "I want", "I don't like") that are brief and to the point
- Co-operative phrases, e.g., "What are your thoughts on this"
- Emphatic statements of interest, e.g., "I would like to"
- Distinction between fact and opinion, e.g., "My experience is different"
- Suggestions without "shoulds" or "oughts" e.g., "How about..." or "Would you like to..."

- Constructive criticism without blame, e.g., "I feel irritated when you interrupt me"
- Seeking others opinions, e.g., "How does this fit in with your ideas"
- Willingness to explore other solutions, e.g., "How can we get around this problem?"

Non-verbal characteristics:

- Receptive listening
- Direct eye contact without staring
- Erect, balanced, open body stance
- Open hand movements
- Smiling when pleased
- Frowning when angry
- Features steady
- Jaw relaxed

Thinking style:

- "I won't allow you to take advantage of me and I won't attack you for being who you are"

The Passive Behavior

They do not express honest feelings, thoughts and beliefs therefore, allow others to violate their rights. They also express thoughts and feelings in an apologetic, self-effacing way so that others easily disregard them. They violate their own rights and sometimes show a subtle lack of respect for the other person's ability to take disappointments, shoulder some responsibility, or handle their own problems.

Verbal characteristics:

- long rambling sentences
- beat-around-the-bush
- hesitant, filled with pauses
- frequent throat clearing

- apologize inappropriately in a soft unsteady voice
- using phrases such as "if it wouldn't be too much trouble…"
- fill in words, e.g., "maybe", "er", "um", "sort of"
- voice often dull and monotonous
- tone may be sing-song or whining
- over-soft or over-warm
- quiet often dropping away
- frequent justifications, e.g., "I wouldn't normally say anything"
- apologies, e.g., "I'm terribly sorry to bother you.."
- qualifiers, e.g., "Its only my opinion" or "I might be wrong"
- self-dismissal, e.g., "It's not important" or "It doesn't really matter"
- self put-downs, e.g., "I'm useless…hopeless" or "You know me…"

Non-verbal characteristics:

- averting gaze
- looking down
- posture can be slouched
- wringing hands
- winking or laughing when expressing anger
- covering mouth with hand
- crossing arms for protection
- ghost smiles when expressing anger or being criticised
- raising eyebrows in anticipation
- jaw trembling
- lip biting

Thinking style:

- "I don't count"
- "My feelings, needs and thoughts are less important than yours"
- "People will think badly of me or not like me"
- "If I say no then I may upset someone, I will be responsible for upsetting them"

The Aggressive Behavior

People with aggressive behavior stand up for their personal rights and express their thoughts, feelings and beliefs in a way that is usually inappropriate and always violates the rights of the other person. People often feel devastated by an encounter with an aggressive person and their superiority is maintained by putting others down. When threatened they usually attack.

Verbal characteristics:

- Strident, sarcastic or condescending voice
- Fluent, few hesitations
- Often abrupt, clipped
- Often fast
- Emphasizing blaming words
- Firm voice
- Tone sarcastic, cold, harsh
- Voice can be strident, often shouting, rising at end
- Use of threats, e.g., "You'd better watch out" or "If you don't..."
- Put downs, e.g., "You've got to be kidding..." or "Don't be so stupid"
- Evaluative comments, emphasizing concepts such as: should", "bad", "ought"
- Sexual / racist remarks
- Boastfulness, e.g., "I haven't got problems like yours"
- Opinions expressed as fact, e.g., "Nobody want to behave like that" or "That's a useless way to do it"
- Threatening questions, e.g., "Haven't you finished that yet?" or "Why on earth did you do it like that?"

Non-verbal characteristics:

- Intruding into the other person's space
- Staring the other person out
- Gestures such as pointing, fist clenching
- Striding around impatiently
- Leaning forward or over
- Crossing arms (unapproachable)

- Smiling may become sneering
- Scowling when angry
- Jaws set firm

Thinking style:

- "I'll get you before you have a chance of getting me"
- "I'm out for number one"
- "The world is a battle ground and I am out to win"

On the basis of these assumptions that people can be categorized on the basis of different patterns of communicating behaviors, I have developed the leadership model called the EI DOSE.

In an organization setting too if we try to categorize people according to behaviors they show via verbal and non verbal communication clues, we end up dividing them into assertive, aggressive and passive employees. There is always another group existing – the 'Mystery' ones who exhibit mysterious combination of all above discussed behavior characteristics. Sometimes they seem to be highly assertive whereas some other time they are absolutely aggressive or passive.

Now when people at workplace are all different, they need to be lead by different leadership styles. Leaders need to devise specific strategies to manage people with varied behaviors. This research proposes the tool of EI DOSE, in form of conceptual 'EI tablets' customized to be applied to employees showing different communication clues at workplace. EI DOSE is nothing but behavioral strategy to manage behaviors of different types. This enunciates that behavior can be managed by behavior itself. However, behavior used to manage other behavior should be properly planned and strategized resulting in most appropriate outcome response.

In order to generate most appropriate solution, research emphasize on integrating principles of communication behaviors, EI and operant conditioning. Reinforcement and punishment, two events that result in changing (increasing or decreasing) specific behaviors are discussed with their positive and negative forms to ensure suitable performance of employees. Term reinforcement is used to strategy that strengthens required behavior whereas punishment weakens unwanted behavior. Brief description of these elements of operant conditioning is as follows:

Positive Reinforcement: Pleasant stimulus is added to strengthen the required behavior

Negative Reinforcement: Reduce or remove unpleasant stimulus to strengthen the required behavior

Positive Punishment: Adding up the unpleasant stimulus to weaken the unwanted behavior

Negative Punishment: Reduce or remove pleasant stimulus to weaken the unwanted behavior

DOSE formulae consists of some assertive behavior ingredients and some aggressive behavior elements combination of which will make perfect EI DOSE to be practiced by leaders to manage behavior of different types. EI DOSE does not include the passive traits of behavior as it is really not the correct way to practice any of the interventions consisting passive behavior elements. It is perceived that leader should always avoid practicing absolute passive or aggressive behavior with his subordinates. Simultaneously, being absolutely assertive always does not work in all situations at workplace. Leader should use specific elements of assertion and aggression to manage his people and make them learn the required behavior. Following elements therefore are included to be the part of EI DOSE:

Assertive Behavior Elements:

1. Showing respect
2. Honesty and fair play
3. Compromise
4. Develop mutuality

Aggressive Behavior Elements:

1. Demanding
2. Ignoring
3. Intimidating
4. Showing violence (shouting, throwing tantrums etc.)

The above mentioned elements are needed to be mixed in specific proportions to make EI DOSE suitable for assertive, aggressive and passive employees.

360 Emotional Intensity (EmIn) is the maximum intensity of the DOSE. Emotional Intensity is set as the measure to evaluate the intensity of behavior elements which are the emotional variables affecting any sort of behavior. In the medicinal products we use mg (milligram) as the medication dosage measurement; likewise we use EmIn (Emotional Intensity) as the emotional dosage measurement for EI DOSE. Due to its qualitative nature, we cannot define emotional intensity in a quantifiable manner as we define one milligram is equal to a thousandth of a gram. 360 EmIn, can be divided equally into eight parts of 45 EmIn each. As per requirement of our formula we need to develop an EI DOSE, combinations of eight behavior elements that make this dosage measurement fits and appropriate to be applied.

EI DOSE for Assertive Behavior

We know now that assertive behavior is characterized by most of the positive behavior elements and people with this behavior are perceived to be the best performers. Although it is not wrong to assume that assertive employees need absolutely an assertive treatment from their leader, there is at least one aggressive behavioral element that needs to be the part of EI DOSE for even most assertive employees in organization. That element is being 'demanding' which can be considered to be the integral part of any behavioral strategy. Primary task of a leader is to get work done by making people follow his instructions. Every leader works for some motives which he wants to fulfill with the help of his subordinates. In order to accomplish all motives in form of goals and objectives, leader has to demand some sort of performance and behavior from all employees. Hence, DOSE recommended for assertive employees is as follows:

EI DOSE Tablet 1- formula consists of:

- ✓ 45 EmIn – Demanding
- ✓ 315 EmIn – Combination of respect, honesty, compromise and mutuality

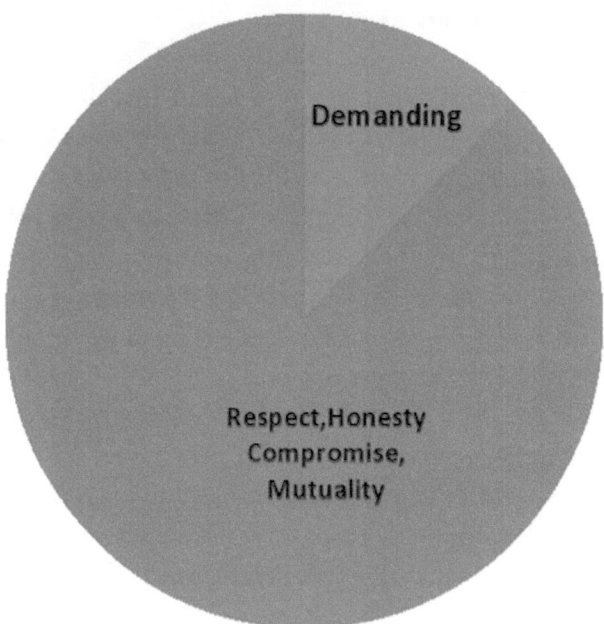

Figure 7 - EI DOSE Tablet 1

Positive Reinforcement: leaders add up the elements of positive behavior in great proportion of 315 EmIn which are likely to motivate employee to the great extent.

Negative Reinforcement: leader ensures the climate where assertive employees are not affected by aggressive or passive behavior of their counterparts.

Positive Punishment: assertive employees also are likely to show unwanted behavior in some specific situations and this is quite obvious as no one in this world is 'perfect'. Even if they do not show that, they are vulnerable to organizational dynamics of power and politics due to which they may not be able to confirm their cent percent performance. In order to reduce this demotivated drive and disengagement, element of 'demand' is added to EI DOSE. By being demanding leader makes sure that assertive employees work consistently assertive way to achieve organizational goals with full of their efficiency.

Negative punishment is not recommended in case of assertive employees.

EI DOSE for Passive Behavior

People with passive behavior lack confidence in their abilities. They usually carry feelings of being unimportant and when they see others getting rewarded for their performance they develop the feeling of jealousy for them. This sort of envy lead them to play politics at workplace. They tend to spread rumors, blame others, pass on secret information, and get sycophant most of the times. This type of negative politics affect overall organizational efficiency and deteriorates the performance of all the employees. It is therefore most important to check this type of behavior and prevent employees either with the use of positive or negative punishment. Word punishment here only means the psychological treatment to reduce unwanted behavior of the employees and not any sort of punitive measures against them. An unpleasant stimulus can be added in form of being more 'demanding' and 'intimidating' with passive people. Suggested formula to treat passive employees at work is represented in form of EI DOSE Tablet 2.

EI DOSE Tablet 2 - formula consists of:

- ✓ 45 EmIn – Demanding
- ✓ 45 EmIn – Intimidating
- ✓ 270 EmIn – Combination of respect, honesty, compromise and mutuality

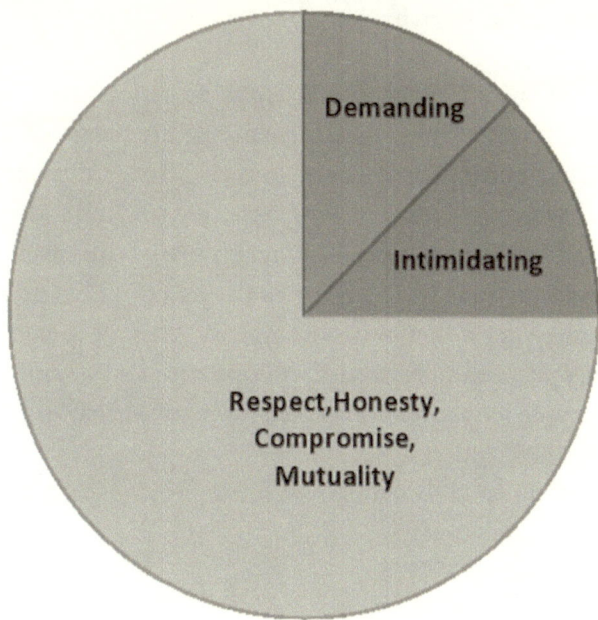

Figure 8 - EI DOSE Tablet 2

Positive Reinforcement: leader practices the elements of positive behavior in good proportion of 270 EmIn which are likely to motivate these employees constantly.

Negative Reinforcement: Passive employees are more vulnerable to criticism and due to weak performance they tend to escalate very slowly in their career. For them leader needs to ensure that they may not get demotivated by lot of criticism and judgments from their counterparts.

Positive Punishment: As discussed earlier passive people perform less efficiently and get involved more in negative politics. In order to reduce this unwanted behavior leader needs to be more intimidating with them to make them sure that this type of behavior will not get entertained at workplace. Simultaneously, he needs to be demanding for consistently better performance. If they will be asked to do more, they will get diverted to positive performance and their tendency to involve into politics will get weaker.

Negative Punishment: Proportion of positive behavior elements gets declined when proportion of negative elements increases. Here 45 EmIn of assertive elements is reduced to discourage the unwanted behavior of passive employees.

EI DOSE for Aggressive Behavior

Aggressive behavior is highly characterized by person's urge to reach to top at any cost, either by hook or crook. These people usually found as involved in shouting, bullying, putting people down, throwing things, demanding, showing off bad moods, swearing, butting in, bossy, ignoring, and intimidating. These are the people who are found to affect entire organizational culture in most negative way. They can do anything or go any extent to beat others and prove themselves the best performers regardless of how competent they are to perform required tasks. These people need to be treated with positive and negative punishment strategies even more serious than suggested for passive behaviors.

EI DOSE Tablet 3 - formula consists of:

- ✓ 45 EmIn – Demanding
- ✓ 45 EmIn – Intimidating
- ✓ 45 EmIn – Ignoring
- ✓ 45 EmIn – Violent
- ✓ 180 EmIn – Combination of respect, honesty, compromise and mutuality

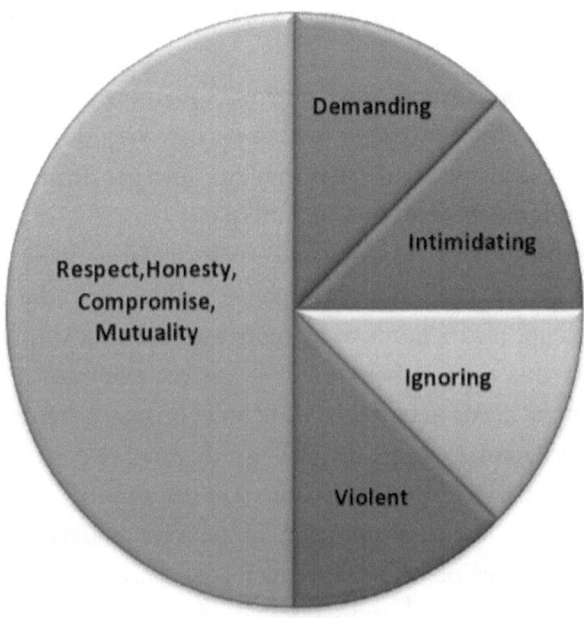

Figure 9 - EI DOSE Tablet 3

Positive Reinforcement: Despite their showing aggression at workplace, leader does not deprive aggressive people fully from assertive behavior elements. He continues (though in lesser intensity) to make them feel receiving respect, honesty, compromise and mutuality from leaders side.

Negative Reinforcement: Leader also tries his level best to create organizational climate where people will be prevented to answer aggression with absolute aggression. Rather they are suggested to treat aggressive counterparts with combination of assertive and aggressive doses than practicing only aggressive behavior elements.

Positive Punishment: In order to reduce aggression related problems, leader should treat aggressive people by being 'demanding', 'intimidating', 'ignoring' and even sometimes being 'violent' (to moderate intensity). Also, it needs to be ensured that violence should not take form of physical violence but should only be practiced in case of aggressive employee showing violence that too in form of maybe, bullying, shouting, throwing tantrums etc.

Negative Punishment: Reducing the intensity of assertive behavior elements like showing respect, honesty & fair play, compromise and mutuality to the great extent can make aggressive people learn lesson about negative consequences of their behavior.

Organizational psychology deals in solving organizational problems caused due to psychological dynamics of individual employees, leaders, groups and teams. Most of the problems are behavior related where employees show the most unwanted and unacceptable behavior. The way in which employees react to various stimuli or situations can be categorized as types of behavior they show at workplace. Leaders usually are found to practice one single approach to treat all his subordinates no matter how different people are with respect to behaviors they show on workplace. It is assumed that performance of employees is outcome of their emotions. When employees who are most assertive and best performers experience to be treated same as those mediocre or below average performers they tend to become highly demotivated and disengaged. Simultaneously if passive or aggressive employees are lead by same assertive leadership approach, problems created by their behavior will not get resolved and organizational performance will suffer. In order to find solution to this problem the intervention of EI DOSE is designed.

EI Dose Summary

In order to fulfill objective of this research focus is set to three specific behaviors to be treated by EI DOSE for effective leadership. The EI DOSE is the leadership model in form of strategy divided into three conceptual EI tablets, the formulas to treat behavioral problems of the employees. The DOSE consists of assertive and aggressive elements to be used in various proportions on people with assertive, passive and aggressive behaviors. EI or Emotional Intelligence is basically used as a tool upon which the EI DOSE is designed. However, practical observation says that in every organization there is always a group or individuals or individual employees who can be considered as having combination of assertive, passive and aggressive traits. This is hence most crucial task for leaders to ascertain the type of behavior person shows and here leader's emotional intelligence helps him to customize the DOSE on the basis of behavioral requirements of the employee. This research is limited to only three common behaviors that can easily be identified by simple observations.

Leadership is all about managing emotions of the people as their performance is directly linked to their emotions. In order to ensure the most efficient performance, employees need to learn appropriate behaviors and this is where the psychological concept of operant conditioning gets involved in this research. This research fundamentally focuses on improving leadership effectiveness by application of EI DOSE which is based upon the psychological foundations of emotional intelligence, behavior, learning and conditioning. This model is expected to strengthen leaders with EI DOSE tool to make employees learn most appropriate behavior and avoiding unwanted behavior through positive/negative reinforcement and punishment. Conceptual measure EmIn (Emotional Intensity) has been initiated to measure the intensity of behavior elements to be added in the DOSE. The model is justified on the foundations of psychology and hence can be implemented by leaders in almost all types of organization setups.

Now, in order to manage this behavior, leaders have to customize EI DOSE, to be implemented to keep this sort of behavior under control. As a matter of fact, EI DOSE implementation totally depends upon the analysis and identification of particular behavior. Going through specific behavior traits and then making proper observations of employee's behavior at workplace can help leader formulate correct EI DOSE combination. Hence EI DOSE can be proved as the efficient initiative to help manage individual behavior at workplace.

Another assumption says that employees who better manage their career and those who are actually satisfied with their career have more productivity than those who are not satisfied with their occupation or profession. Unsatisfied employees show frustration at work, they delay the tasks, have lesser productivity and hence they finally affect business performance. Emotional intelligence principles can again be taken into consideration when it comes to career planning, development and management.

EI and Career Development

Another research 'Structured Emotional Career Counseling and Career Development'[75] conducted on use of EI in career counseling produced important insights about how by using EI, career counselors can help their clients make right career decisions.

It is always crucial yet most important time when student selects any vocation as career to pursue for lifetime. Selection of wrong alternative this time may make entire life miserable. At the time of selecting field of specialization, psyche of student revolves around number of factors to choose particular option. Fundamentally, counselors suggest areas which they find very much 'in fashion' and where they see more chances of career growth and development. That time student finds that alternative suitable due to tempting packages and urge to achieve esteemed status. Finally candidate starts taking interest in that particular area. But this type of interest is always time bound as it is been generated and synthesized keeping other motivators in mind ignoring emotional satisfaction of the individual. Further, counselors focus on certain other aspects too while counseling. They assess individual personalities, their skill sets, their competencies, interests etc. and do not focus on individual emotional needs.

Much of emphasis though is given to individual's personality during career counseling it is found in recent studies that even personalities get change over time. The researchers, of the University of Manchester's School of Psychological

Sciences found during their study that personalities can and do change. According to them personality changes relates much more strongly to changes in life satisfaction. Their study clears how changes to our circumstances, such as a higher income, getting married or a different job might influence our wellbeing which finally changes some or many of our personality attributes.[76]

Changes to attributes of personality also are the results of the emotions we experience. Extent to which we encounter positive or negative emotions determine how and what sort of personality attributes will get affected and changed. Similarly as discussed in previous sections interests of a person could also be time bound. Area in which person finds his motives get fulfilled, he starts taking interest in that which is highly artificial and synthesized process. Skills, competencies, abilities all can get learned and unlearned but there is one aspect with every human being that never changes and that is his tendency to get emotional and experience variety of positive, negative, primary and secondary emotions. Human's success in every role depends upon how emotionally he is satisfied with tasks he performs and reward he receives from that role. If selected vocation is aligned with human's personality, skills, interests or competencies, and he is coming across negative emotions in that job, he will not be able to soar high in career of that specific domain.

The survey conducted during the research advocates how professionals in various vocations agree to the fact that emotions have got great significance in career success and development. Further, they admitted that during the process of career counseling, those vocations should be recommended wherein individual experiences highest levels of emotional satisfaction. On these findings the structured emotional intelligence questionnaire was developed as a suggestive tool using which counselors can easily discover areas where candidate experience positive emotions. This study generated new stimulus and opened new areas of investigation as to how emotions are significant to career counseling and career development.

Organizations should also, at the time of selecting the employees ensure that whether employee is an emotional fit to the job or not. Simple meaning of this is - will employee be happy doing what he is given as the job task? It is also true that an employee cannot always love every task he is given by the employer but at least he should be emotionally satisfied by core tasks he is expected to perform. This sounds not relevant to some people but thinking deeply on significance of emotional satisfaction for career growth, gives you lot of insights about well being of employee and employer both.

Today's business scenario is highly complex due to strong competition amongst business entities functioning on the global platform. Companies spend exorbitant amounts on research and development to find out ways to excel over their competitors. They implement different strategies to achieve competitive advantage yet there are certain similarities in approaches they use to compete. Business is considered as the concern - of the people, for the people and by the people and hence success or failure of the business is completely based upon level of cooperation 'people' provide to specific business. These people, who have direct or indirect association with business, are called as stakeholders and they have strong impact on the success of business they are related to. When we talk of managing these stakeholders there is one common approach most of the successful companies are found to have adopted and that is 'emotionally intelligent strategies'. Although they do not specifically mention anywhere to use this term but if you see closely and study their patterns and processes to attract stakeholders you will find how these companies use emotional intelligence to devise all their strategies. In all functional areas of business at least some level of emotional intelligence is required and in some specific areas it is much more significant. This book is expected to help new and small entrepreneurs to benchmark their strategies with fortune 500 companies who have used emotional intelligence as great tool to achieve competitive advantage and sustainable growth.

Endnotes

1 Howard Gardener, The Nine Types of Intelligence available at: http://skyview.vansd.org/lschmidt/Projects/The%20Nine%20Types%20of%20Intelligence.html

2 Psychology.about.com 2013-09-1, Theories of Emotion, available at: http://psychology.about.com/od/psychologytopics/a/theories-of-emotion.htm

3 Scherer, K. R. 2005. What are emotions? And how can they be measured?. Social Science Information 44: 693–727

4 The World Islamic Propagation Establishment (UK), You must know this Man, available at: http://www.themodernreligion.com/prophet/prophet_know.htm

5 Ibid

6 Ibid

7 Forbes, 21 Quotes from Henry Ford on Business, Leadership and Life, available at: http://www.forbes.com/sites/erikaandersen/2013/05/31/21-quotes-from-henry-ford-on-business-leadership-and-life/

8 Walmart (n.d) An Introduction to Walmart.com available at: http://www.walmart.com/cp/An-Introduction-to-Walmart.com/542413

9 Tata Steel 2013, About Us, available at: http://www.tatasteel.com/about-us/company-profile.asp

10 Tata Steel 2013 Vision and Mission available at: http://www.tatasteelindia.com/corporate/vision-and-strategy.asp

11 Walmart 2013 Walmart Purpose available at: www.walmartstores.com/AboutUs/8123.aspx

12 BP 2013 Our Values, available at: http://www.bp.com/en_no/norway/sustainability/our-values.html

13 British Petroleum 2013 Our Values available at: http://www.bp.com/en/global/corporate/about-bp/company-information/our-values.html

14 Samsung 2013 Samsung Philosophy, Vision 2020 available at: http://www.samsung.com/us/aboutsamsung/samsung_group/values_and_philosophy/

15 Samsung Electronics 2013 Corporate Ethics available at :http://www.samsung.com/us/aboutsamsung/sustainability/sustainablemanagement/download/SamsungValueCode_ofConduct.pdf

16 Toyota 2013, Guiding Principles at Toyota available at: http://www.toyota-global.com/company/vision_philosophy/guiding_principles.html

17 Tata Steel 2010, Performance through Sustainability available at: http://www.tatasteel.com/investors/annual-report-2010-11/html/hd4.html

18 Tata Steel 2013 Corporate Citizenship, Environment available at: http://www.tatasteel.com/corporate-citizenship/environment.asp

19 Walmart, 2013 Global Responsibility Report, available at: http://az204679.vo.msecnd.net/media/documents/updated-2013-global-responsibility-report_130113953638624649.pdf

20 Ibid

21 Ibid

22 British Petroleum 2012 Building a Stronger and Safer BP, Sustainability Review 2012, available at: http://www.bp.com/content/dam/bp/pdf/sustainability/group-reports/BP_Sustainability_Review_2012.pdf

23 Ibid

24 Samsung Electronics 2012 Sustainability Report, available at: http://www.samsung.com/us/aboutsamsung/sustainability/sustainabilityreports/download/2012/2012_sustainability_rpt.pdf

25 Ibid

26 Toyota, Toyota's CSR Concepts, available at: http://www.toyota-global.com/sustainability/csr_initiatives/csr_concepts/policy.html

27 Tata Steel, 100th Annual Report 2006 – 2007, available at: http://www.tatasteel.com/investors/pdf/100-annualreport.pdf

28 Walmart, Walmart Releases 2013 Annual Shareholders' Meeting Materials. April 22, 2013, available at: http://news.walmart.com/news-archive/2013/04/22/walmart-releases-2013-annual-shareholders-meeting-materials

29 Ibid

30 Walmart 2013 Annual Report available at: http://c46b2bcc0db5865f5a76-91c2ff8eba65983a1c33d367b8503d02.r78.cf2.rackcdn.com/88/2d/4f df67184a359fdef07b1c3f4732/2013-annual-report-for-walmart-stores-inc_130221024708579502.pdf

31 Ibid

32 British Petroleum, Annual Report and Form 20-F 2012, available at: http://www.bp.com/content/dam/bp/pdf/investors/BP_Annual_Report_and_Form_20F_2012.pdf

33 2012 Samsung Electronics Annual Report, available at: http://www.samsung.com/us/aboutsamsung/investor_relations/financial_information/downloads/2013/SECAR2012_Eng_Final.pdf

34 Ibid

35 Toyota Motors, Relations with Shareholders, Making Efforts toward Continual Improvements to Accomplish Solid Profitability, and Making Better Cars, available at: http://www.toyota-global.com/sustainability/csr_initiatives/stakeholders/shareholders/

36 Ibid

37 Toyota Motor Corporation – Annual Report 2012, available at: http://www.toyota-global.com/investors/ir_library/annual/pdf/2012/ar12_e.pdf

38 Tata Steel – The world of steel brochure available at: http://www.tatasteel.com/media/pdf/group-brochure.pdf

39 Tata Steel 105th Annual Report 2011 – 2012, available at: http://www.tatasteeleurope.com/file_source/Functions/Finance/Documents/annual-report-2011-12.pdf

40 Ibid

41 Tata Steel, Marketing Innovations. available at: http://www.tatasteelindia.com/corporate/innovations/marketing-innovations-brands.asp

42 ICMR, Lessons in Customer Service from Wal-Mart, available at: http://www.icmrindia.org/casestudies/catalogue/Marketing/Lessons%20in%20Customer%20Service%20from%20Wal-Mart.htm#Introduction

43 Ibid

44 Kim Bhasin, Business Insider, BP Is Spending $500 Million To Fix Its Brand And Get Everybody To Forget About Deepwater Horizon, available at: http://www.businessinsider.com/bp-is-spending-500-million-to-fix-its-brand-and-get-everybody-to-forget-about-deepwater-horizon-2012-2

45 Customers, Samsung SDI, available at: http://www.samsungsdi.com/sustain/s2_3_1t.jsp

46 Ibid

47 Toyota, Relations with Customers available at: http://www.toyota-global.com/sustainability/csr_initiatives/stakeholders/customers/quality.html

48 Ibid

49 Ibid

50 Tata Steel, Our HR policies are customised to local and global requirements, Hindu Business Line August 15, 2012 available at: http://www.tata.in/media/reports/inside.aspx?artid=FV+QYGwmkOY=

51 Ibid

52 Ibid

53 Ibid

54 Michael Bergdahl 2010 'How the HR division at Wal-Mart drives the company's success through people' hrmagazine.co.uk, available at: http://www.hrmagazine.co.uk/hro/analysis/1018448/how-hr-division-wal-mart-drives-companys-success-people

55 Walmart, Working at Walmart available at: http://careers.walmart.com/about-us/working-at-walmart/

56 Ibid

57 British Petroleum. Working at BP. available at: http://www.bp.com/en/global/corporate/careers/working-at-bp.html

58 Ibid

59 British Petroleum Sustainability Review 2012 available at: http://www.bp.com/content/dam/bp/pdf/sustainability/group-reports/BP_Sustainability_Review_2012.pdf

60 Ibid

61 Ibid

62 Ibid

63 Ibid

64 Samsung Electronics, 2011 Sustainability Report, available at: http://www.samsung.com/us/aboutsamsung/ir/corporategovernance/corporatesocialresponsibility/download/2011Environmentalnsocialreport.pdf

65 Ibid

66 Ibid

67 Ibid

68 Toyota Motors, Relations with Employees available at: http://www.toyota-global.com/sustainability/csr_initiatives/stakeholders/employees/index3.html

69 Ibid

70 Husain Sehba. '360 Degree EI Implementation Business Model – Tool to Achieve Competitive Advantage for Small, Medium and New Enterprises', International Journal of Management (IJM), Volume 4, Issue 3, May – June 2013 ISSN 0976 6502. pp. 38-47

71 Shaw, Robert, Computer Aided Marketing & Selling (1991) Butterworth Heinemann ISBN 978-0-7506-1707-9

72 Richard. E. Boyatzis 2009, Competencies as a Behavioral Approach to Emotional Intelligence, Journal of Management Development, Emerald Group Publishing Limited, 0262-1711 Vol. 28 No. 9, pp. 749-770

73 Goleman, D. 1998, Working with Emotional Intelligence, Bantam Books, New York, NY

74 Dulwich College Suzhou (n.d) The Characteristics of Passive, Aggressive and Assertive Communication available at: http://www.dulwich-suzhou.cn/uploaded/DCSZ_meet_the_counselor/The_Characteristics_of_Passive,_Aggressive_and_Assertive_Communication.pdf

75 Sehba Husain, 'Structured Emotional Career Counseling and Career Development' International Journal of Research in Commerce and Management, Volume 4 (2013), Issue 9 ISSN 0976 – 2183, pp 66-74

76 Christopher J. Boyce, Alex M. Wood, Nattavudh Powdthavee (2013) Is Personality Fixed? Personality Changes as Much as "Variable" Economic Factors and More Strongly Predicts Changes to Life Satisfaction, Social Indicators Research March 2013, Volume 111, Issue 1, pp 287-305